THE HISTORY *of* AUSTRALIAN WINE

THE HISTORY *of* AUSTRALIAN WINE

STORIES FROM THE VINEYARD TO THE CELLAR DOOR
1900–2000

MAX ALLEN

 VICTORY BOOKS

VICTORY BOOKS
An imprint of Melbourne University Publishing Limited
187 Grattan Street, Carlton, Victoria 3053, Australia
mup-info@unimelb.edu.au
www.mup.com.au
First published 2012
Text copyright © Max Allen, 2012
Design and typography © Melbourne University Publishing Limited, 2012

Text designed by Philip Campbell Design
Cover designed by Philip Campbell Design
Printed by ABC in China

National Library of Australia Cataloguing-in-Publication entry:

Allen, Max, 1968-

The History of Australian Wine / Max Allen.

9780522856149 (hbk.)
Includes index.
Wine and wine making—Australia.

641.220994

Previous: Barrels of wine and cartons of Brandivino being loaded onto a truck outside the Yalumba headquarters

Opposite: Yalumba pickers, 1954 vintage

Pages vi–vii: Coldstream Hills in the Yarra Valley

Pages x–xi: Penfolds Magill Estate

CONTENTS

FOREWORD

This is a unique book about people from various walks of life who have achieved success. They are passionate and dedicated to their profession. Their stories are the result of many years of hard work by noted historian Rob Linn, who interviewed key pioneers from all regions of Australia affiliated with the Australian wine and grape growing industry.

Rob's work was commissioned by the Wolf Blass Foundation. The interviews are now a rare and valuable oral history held in the State Records of South Australia. Author Max Allen has based *The History of Australian Wine* on that oral history, adding his own contributions to develop a comprehensive and enjoyable book on the Australian wine industry, with particular emphasis on its more recent formative years when it bloomed from a producer of fortified wines to become the fourth biggest wine export country and supplier of high-class, quality table wines in the world.

I was privileged to build my own company during that period of transition, and enjoyed playing my part in that success. However, this is not a book about Wolf Blass—it is a unique book of record from the voices of those who, in their own and differing ways, contributed to the history and development of our great industry.

Through the Wolf Blass Foundation, which has funded this long, and at times difficult, project, I believe I have been able to give the Australian wine industry a legacy that is unique in the world, and one that will endure and provide an invaluable source of historical information for years to come. It is important that we record for posterity the history of our industry. It is particularly satisfying that we have been able to do so interviewing key figures while they were alive. It is not often that history is recorded by those who made it.

It has been my very great pleasure to have facilitated the publication of this book through the Wolf Blass Foundation.

I invite you to enjoy *The History of Australian Wine*.

Wolf Blass AM BVK
November 2011

INTRODUCTION

[Australia has] gone from being a fortified wine industry to a table wine industry; from a domestic table wine industry to being a global table wine industry. [It used to be] an industry that made wine by accident … These days it's an industry that makes wine by design.

BRIAN CROSER

History runs in cycles. Sometimes you get to see one of those cycles up close, from beginning to end.

I started drinking wine twenty-five years ago. My introductory bottle was (as it was for many, many others) Brown Brothers Spatlese Lexia, a sweet, golden fluid filled with the mellow sunshine of late autumn. This stuff was brilliant; it, and the bottles that came in quick succession, ignited a passion for Australian wine that continues to this day.

Little did I know then that, as I was falling in love with its products, the Australian wine industry itself was—in the memorable words of viticulturist Di Davidson—'on the bones of its bum'.

Back then, in the mid 1980s, the industry was lumbered with a massive grape glut; supply outweighed demand so heavily that the South Australian government sponsored a vine-pull scheme, encouraging growers to rip out their vineyards; discounting was rife; the wineries were enduring a huge round of buyouts and consolidation; export markets were virtually nonexistent.

I was a newbie, then, of course. Blissfully unaware of the industry's woes, I just kept on searching insatiably for new wines. But my burgeoning interest soon morphed into a career path—first working in bottle shops, then a couple of stints in a winery during vintage, finally a job as a wine writer. And the closer I got to the industry, the more I became aware of the changes it was going through.

Only one thing saddens a winemaker more than a teetotaller.

A drunk

Making a wine is a labour of love.
From looking after the vines to picking
to making the wine to waiting for each vinta
But all this labour is well worth it for
pleasures.
Someone once wrote that
without sunshine.
We tend to agree.
Whether it's the c
savouring of a good p
sense of well-being.
So naturally we're
these pleasures.
But it's a free countr
Far better than that

Above: Yalumba managing director Robert Hill Smith in front of a smart drinking campaign poster

I watched as confidence grew, as the export juggernaut picked up speed, as countless new vineyards and wineries opened across the country, and as the industry rose to spectacular heights of success at the end of the 1990s. And then, during the first decade of this century, I watched as confidence gave way to complacency, as boom led to bust, as a bloated industry descended into today's despondency of oversupply, export stagnation and corporate consolidation.

In other words, in the twenty-five years that I've known it, Australian wine has, in many ways, come full circle.

This book takes in a much broader view than the past twenty-five years, though. It tells the story of Australian wine during the entire twentieth century. And what a cyclical story it has been.

Based on a series of interviews conducted across a wide range of industry figures—from winemakers to cellar hands, from business leaders to grape growers—it's neither an official history nor a definitive history; it's an oral history, full of first-hand accounts of what happened when and why, and personal opinions on how Australian wine got to where it is today.

Cycles straddle the century. As I have said, we have come full circle in many ways. For example, Australia was a major exporter of wine in the early years of the twentieth century—and by the end of the century, after decades of hiatus, it was again. Likewise, for the first half of the century Australia's wine family companies dominated the industry—and now, as the large corporations that ran the show during the 1990s and 2000s fracture and fragment, the family-owned companies are returning to the fore.

There are also many tales here about the irreversible changes that have occurred over those 100 years, such as our evolving from a nation of sweet sherry drinkers to a nation infatuated with crisp sauvignon blanc.

Yalumba managing director Robert Hill Smith—whose family was already three generations into its winemaking history when the twentieth century began—sums up perfectly perhaps the most profound development: 'The biggest change,' he says, '[has been] the international recognition for the quality of Australian viticulture, Australian winemaking, Australian marketing, Australian research in wine … It's exciting. It's brought youth to the industry. It's brought youth to country regions. It's brought terrific economic benefits to communities that were struggling with crops, and businesses in general that really didn't have a competitive advantage internationally. And that's been a great thing for Australia and the country.'

It's not all positive stories, though, by any means. No matter where in the century you land, you will find tension threading through everyday conversation: ongoing antagonism between the wine industry and the government of the day; the symbiotic yet often distrustful relationship between grape-growers and their customers, the wineries; and the underlying dichotomy of Australian culture— on one hand wowserish and prurient, on the other debauched and indulgent.

There are plenty of larrikins, pioneers and characters among the storytellers here, from charismatic leaders who have carefully mentored the next generation and imbued the Australian wine community with a strong sense of collaboration and mateship, to bloody-minded individuals who fiercely steered their own course and yet, ironically, inspired many with their iconoclasm and pig-headedness. It's fascinating to trace the networks of influence across geographical and generational space.

At the heart of it all, though, running like a constant soundtrack to the century, beats a powerful sense of resilience. Australian vignerons have always faced challenges—lack of water, excessive heat, the tyranny of distance—and much of this country's wine story is about how those challenges have been overcome at a day-to-day level.

But it has been in times of extreme adversity, during environmental, financial or global crisis, that the industry has taken its biggest leaps forward.

This is the most important lesson that can be learned from the stories collected here. Take that glum period of the mid 1980s that I mentioned earlier.

For every tale of woe and heartache recorded here, there is another recounting hope. At the same time that unwanted vines were being pulled from the ground in the Barossa, for example, a group of Masters of Wine, visiting from the UK, were working themselves into a lather of excitement over the wines they were tasting in the region's cellars—an excitement that would go on to help fuel the subsequent export boom.

As well as illuminating the past, a knowledge of history can guide us through the present. So, while the Australian wine industry is undoubtedly going through a very tough time at the moment, the stories in this book remind us that, just as the seeds of Australia's export wine boom were sown during a time of domestic crisis in the mid 1980s, so the seeds of a domestic revival are being sown right now, in direct response to global challenges. You need only look around: new, enthusiastic winemakers are emerging all the time, doing amazing things— reinventing old styles, introducing new ones, going out on a limb, being fearless, experimenting, and making sure they share their enthusiasm through social media.

Despite the doom and gloom at a broader industry level, there has never been more reason to be excited about the grassroots.

In his interview, writer, winemaker and judge James Halliday muses about the magical ability of wine to store memory—to pour history into your glass after years of quietly slumbering in the cellar. He could have been talking about the words and stories that he and many others shared and that are collected in this book: 'It's just wonderful to have something that you can link to the past [but] also know that there is a future, that people will be looking back in fifty years' time on the events and wines of today.'

I would like to personally acknowledge the incredible effort and dedication over many years of historian Rob Linn in recording, transcribing and compiling the interviews on which this book is based. Rob harvested the stories, fermented them and carefully bottled them up. I have merely decanted them onto the page.

Opposite: Writer, winemaker and judge James Halliday

In the fifties when you went to dinner you had sherry as an aperitif, beer with the meal and perhaps a port after the meal. Today, [you] have a glass of wine at any time … [This is not] only a difference, but a revolution.

GUENTER PRASS

Wouldn't it be fantastic to step into a time machine and hurl yourself back to when our great-grandparents were young, and to drink the wines they enjoyed? You can, of course—although it's an increasingly expensive exercise—drink wines today that were made before you were born: dusty old bottles of Grange from the early 1960s; rare Coonawarra 'clarets' from the 1950s; luscious, treacly Rutherglen muscats from the 1920s, with their impenetrable olive-black colour in the glass, impossibly intense and toothachingly sweet. It's possible, if you have a lazy $1000 about your person, to buy a bottle of 100-year-old Para from Seppeltsfield: extraordinary tawny 'port' that was made in the year 1910. But these are all *old* wines, their flavours moulded by the hands of time, their tastes carved by the interaction of the alcohol and the acids and the grape-skin extract as they have slumbered, in barrel and bottle, for decades.

No, I'm talking about tasting these wines in their first flush of youth, when they were (mostly) meant to be drunk. Wouldn't it be amazing to sit in a dark, gas-lit wine saloon in north-east Victoria in the years before World War I, the memory of the gold rush and bushrangers still fresh in the minds of the people around you, sipping on a small, chunky glass of Fourpenny Dark port; to save up during the lean 1930s for a bottle of Houghton White Burgundy, a light white to liven up a meagre picnic on the banks of the Swan River; to be one of the few who knew about the mad French-Irishman making some of the world's greatest red wines in

THE HISTORY OF AUSTRALIAN WINE

a dirt-floor shack in the Hunter Valley in the early 1940s; to seek consolation in a bottle of Chestnut Teal sherry during the darkest years of World War II; to be one of the first to experience the bright sparkling sweetness of Barossa Pearl in the mid 1950s; to take a flagon of claret to a party during the height of the swinging sixties.

Wine styles can define an era just as much as fashion, music, movies and food. To mangle gastronome Jean Anthelme Brillat-Savarin's famous aphorism: tell me what you drink and I will tell you where you are in time. Australia witnessed some dramatic changes in its drinking habits during the twentieth century, from fortifieds and Germanic-style 'moselles' to reds, to whites and back to reds, with both brief and extended crazes for sparkling wines, rosé, coolers and everything in between. And now, at the beginning of the twenty-first century, we're experiencing deja vu: Australia's top fortified wines have gained the international respect they deserve, and Germanic-style white wines are back in fashion. To borrow the title of a song from that other great philosopher, Justin Timberlake: what goes around comes around.

A Victorian legacy: Fourpenny Dark and Empire Port

Fourpenny Dark. Sounds a bit frightening, really, doesn't it? I imagine a thick liquid, the colour of boot polish, with a sweet but not altogether pleasant aroma of slightly stale raisins, and a claggy, hot taste to match. This was the kind of rough fortified wine that sustained the wine industry in the very early years of last century: despite some remarkable table wines being made in cooler climates like those of the Yarra Valley and Geelong, and warmer places like McLaren Vale and the Barossa, during the second half of the nineteenth century, the majority of Australians had developed a taste for strong fortified wines such as sweet sherry. Australia also shipped a vast quantity of fortifieds, and heavy, 'ferruginous' dry reds that tasted like sucking on an iron bar, to the motherland during the first few decades of the twentieth century: Empire Port, much of which found its way to dusty, smoky pubs in the north of England, where it was mixed with lemonade to temper its fire, came from the colonies.

We know what Fourpenny Dark was made from, because Bob Hollick from Mildara remembers his father having to plant vineyards in Mildura to keep up with demand:

It was after the First World War that shiraz and grenache became prominent in the district here from the soldier settlement and the local winery. The Mildara group was the only winery in the district. They wanted the shiraz and the grenache to make what they used to call, in those days, Fourpenny Dark.

These wines often wouldn't have tasted all that fabulous—certainly not to today's drinkers, used to cleanly made, fault-free, fresh wines. The lack of cooling and poor understanding of the effect of bacteria on wine spoilage would have resulted in heavy, clumsy, often stale wines. Indeed, it was the desire to clean up and ensure the stability of Australia's fortified wines—especially those destined for export—that initially drove much of the research and innovation in the wine industry during the rest of the century.

A sweet spot: the 1930s and Hamilton's Ewell Moselle and Yalumba's Carte d'Or

Reading this now, in the early twenty-first century, you, dear reader, take cool-fermented wines—wines picked early and fermented cool to retain crisp acidity and freshness, and bottled with a lick of residual sugar to balance the zestiness—for granted. And if you have a look on the shelves of your local fine wine merchant or on the list at a trendy wine bar, you'll see that 'Germanic' style cool-fermented rieslings are all the rage these days. This is nothing new. Australian wine drinkers have long had an on-again, off-again love for off-dry or medium-sweet white wines modelled on the rieslings of Germany, a love affair that started back in the early years of the twentieth century.

In 1929, Syd Hamilton travelled to Europe and witnessed the enormous improvements that could be made to white wines by chilling the fermenting juice. So he installed an ammonia refrigeration plant at his family's winery southwest of Adelaide, and ran chilled brine through copper pipes in the must (crushed grape juice). Hamilton's winemaker, Russian-born John Speck, used the cooling process to produce a light, white table wine named Ewell Moselle. Like almost all wines of the time, it was labelled generically: 'moselle' is a variant of Mosel, the German river whose steep banks are planted with riesling vineyards. This, and another riesling called Carte d'Or, developed by the young Austrian winemaker Rudi Kronberger at Yalumba, would become one of the most popular brands of the decade among the minority of people who bought table wines, and helped wean many drinkers off sweet sherry.

Some other producers, such as the Emu Wine Company at Morphett Vale, realised the potential of refrigeration and successfully used the technique to improve the quality of light, dry sherry, but few adopted it for table wines—simply because the demand wasn't there.

Some reliable and relatively popular table wines such as Lindemans Cawarra Claret were produced at this time, and Jack Mann was making the first vintages of that old stalwart, Houghton White Burgundy, using Swan Valley chenin blanc grapes over in Western Australia. But the overwhelming majority—80 to 90 per cent—of the Australian wine market was sweet whites, sherries and port, and would remain that way for another two decades.

Above: Legendary Hunter Valley winemaker, Maurice O'Shea

Opposite: Fortified wine and brandy labels from the first half of the twentieth century

In 1937, Maurice O'Shea made what he regarded as one of his greatest red wines from old shiraz vines at Mount Pleasant in the Hunter Valley. The 1937 Mountain A Dry Red was made in a dirt-floor shack with no electricity and yet, by all accounts, was remarkable. At the time, hardly anyone in the country knew wine like this existed, let alone appreciated it. When he tasted it almost fifty years later, James Halliday described it as 'the perfect wine … a wine that will live with me for the rest of my days'.

Imagine what that wine tasted like when it was young. Just *imagine*.

Autumn Brown and Chestnut Teal: fortifieds from the 1940s

Despite talented winemakers such as O'Shea at Mount Pleasant, Jack Mann at Houghton, Roger Warren at Hardys and Colin Preece at Seppelt's Great Western producing some of this country's most extraordinary table wines during and just after World War II (the 1946 Seppelt Sparkling Burgundy is one of the most profound old wines I've ever drunk), the popularity of fortifieds persisted throughout the 1940s and 1950s. When Guenter Prass arrived in Australia in 1955 to work for Orlando, his recollection of what he saw reads like the display in a typical wine shop of the period:

Orlando Yellow Label Sweet Sherry, Orlando Conto Port, McWilliam's Cream Sherry, McWilliam's Royal Reserve Sweet Sherry, Yalumba Autumn Brown Sweet Sherry, Mildara Chestnut Teal, Lindemans Montillo, Penfolds Club Port, just to name a few. The blends were made in big volumes—sweet sherry from sultana and muscat, port from grenache, mataro, shiraz. There was also quite a considerable export market for these wines to the UK and Canada; I remember big shipments of Sweet Red of 42 Proof and Sweet Red of NE 27 Proof. A shipment of these wines got stuck in the Suez Canal, which was closed for British and French ships for a number of years after the 1956 Suez War. During all that time the Australian Sweet Red was maturing in the Egyptian heat … The insurance companies paid out the shippers and five, six years later the wines were auctioned on the UK market. I tasted some of the blends; they certainly had improved substantially compared to the original wines!

As the resilience of these wines stranded in Suez demonstrates, the quality of Australian fortifieds had improved in the 1940s, thanks to the sterling efforts of wine scientists such as John Fornachon and Ray Beckwith, and winemakers such as Max Schubert at Penfolds, who was sent to Europe at the end of the decade to learn more about sherry production—but came back with a dream of making a very different wine.

Orlando
Gold Medal
LIQUEUR MUSCAT
SELECTED AUSTRALIAN WINE
BOTTLED BY
G. GRAMP & SONS LTD
ORLANDO VINEYARDS STH AUSTRALIA
NET 1 PINT 6 FLUID OZS

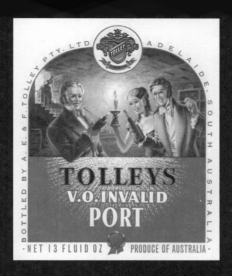

BOTTLED BY A. E. & F. TOLLEY PTY. LTD · ADELAIDE · SOUTH AUSTRALIA
TOLLEYS
V.O. INVALID
PORT
· NET 13 FLUID OZ · PRODUCE OF AUSTRALIA ·

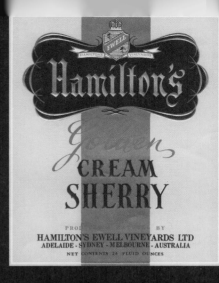

Hamilton's
Golden
CREAM
SHERRY
PRODUCED BY
HAMILTON'S EWELL VINEYARDS LTD
ADELAIDE · SYDNEY · MELBOURNE · AUSTRALIA
NET CONTENTS 26 FLUID OUNCES

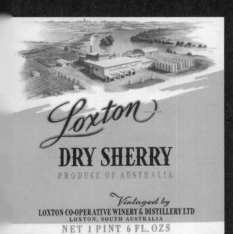

Loxton
DRY SHERRY
PRODUCE OF AUSTRALIA
Vintaged by
LOXTON CO-OPERATIVE WINERY & DISTILLERY LTD
LOXTON, SOUTH AUSTRALIA
NET 1 PINT 6 FL. OZS

SEPPELT
Long Neck Brandy
NET 1 PINT 6 FL. OZ
DISTILLED & BOTTLED BY B. SEPPELT & SONS PTY. LTD. AUSTRALIA

HAMILTON'S
FOUNDED 1837   EWELL   FOUNDED 1837
Special Port
BOTTLED BY HAMILTON'S EWELL VINEYARDS LTD GLENELG. S.A.
· NET HALF IMPERIAL GALLON ·

Toora Vale
SPECIAL
MUSCAT
Bottled by the makers
TOORA VALE CO. LTD
BERRI · RIVER MURRAY
SOUTH AUSTRALIA
NETT CONTENTS 26 FLUID OUNCES

CHATEAU TANUNDA
BRANDY
FINE MATURED BRANDY
B. SEPPELT & SONS LIMITED
181 FLINDERS STREET
ADELAIDE
SOUTH AUSTRALIA
150 ml 37·5% ALC/VOL
PRODUCE OF
AUSTRALIA

Loxton
OLOROSO
SHERRY
PRODUCE OF AUSTRALIA
Vintaged by
LOXTON CO-OPERATIVE WINERY & DISTILLERY LTD
LOXTON, SOUTH AUSTRALIA
NET 1 PINT 6 FL. OZS

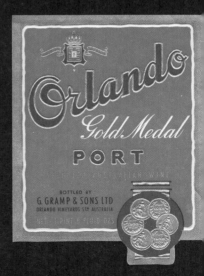

Orlando
Gold Medal
PORT
SELECTED AUSTRALIAN WINE
BOTTLED BY
G. GRAMP & SONS LTD
ORLANDO VINEYARDS STH AUSTRALIA
NET 1 PINT 6 FLUID OZS

Table wines take off: Orlando Riesling, Ben Ean Moselle and Barossa Pearl in the 1950s

In 1953, Orlando became the first Australian company to produce a riesling using new German cool-fermented pressure tank technology. And the fresh, lively, *modern* white wine was a revelation.

Melbourne retailer Doug Crittenden realised immediately how popular it would be with a new generation of post-war wine drinkers. He remembers Keith Gramp of Orlando showing him the wine before it was released:

I tasted it and I said, 'Keith, this is very close to German-style riesling.' We'd never seen anything like it in Australia. I said, 'Is there any chance that I could pre-sell some of this before you release it to see how much I can sell?' And I made up a brochure, wrote out how it was tasting and what I thought—it was one of the finest rieslings I'd ever seen and tasted in Australia. I offered it to people to buy a half-dozen or a dozen. And we sent this circular out to all our customers. And sight unseen, and before they'd even seen a bottle, or before they'd even seen a label of it, I sold two hundred dozen. It was unheard of. Orlando could not believe it. I got the first release. Well, after that, it was rationed to the trade.

The extraordinary success of Orlando's riesling inspired Ray Kidd at Lindemans to develop a similar-style wine. Lindemans already had a good market for red table wines such as Cawarra claret—despite the fact that most people drank fortifieds—and did good business with hotels across New South Wales. Ray Kidd believed the time was right for something new:

In '56 I decided that there was a big swing to table wine—and it was sweet sherry drinkers transferring over. We used to do very extensive public tastings, so we kept heavily in contact with the general public. Not just the connoisseurs, or anything like that. We would have big tastings in the cellars, through hotels. And hotels would invite all their customers … table wine was way down here and fortified wines were still high.

There were moselles on the market. Every company had a moselle with ghastly imitation German labels. I reckoned that I could do a hell of a lot better than that and I literally invented and launched Ben Ean Moselle. Even designed the label for it. It was just what a great mass of people wanted. It was a great product.

But the wine that captured the imagination of Australians more spectacularly than any other in the 1950s was Orlando's Barossa Pearl.

Above: For most of the twentieth century, Australian wine was labeled with generic European names rather than the name of the grape variety

THE HISTORY OF AUSTRALIAN WINE

Colin Gramp and Guenter Prass modelled Barossa Pearl on the *Perlwein* style so popular in Germany. Colin was certain that the wine's 'delicate yet fruity character, together with the light effervescence produced by the natural and controlled fermentation of its own sweetness, would make it a wine of great appeal'.[1] The bottle for the new product was modelled on that used for Perrier mineral water, sealed with a screwcap, featuring a chartreuse and chocolate–coloured label and capsule created by designer Wytt Morro.

On 5 November 1956, not long after the Melbourne Olympic Games had taken Australia by storm, the first bottles of Barossa Pearl emerged from the bottling line at Rowland Flat. Nothing prepared Orlando for what followed.

'It developed like an avalanche,' says Guenter Prass. 'And for many, many years it was restricted. I mean, we couldn't make as much as people wanted. After we bottled ten million bottles we gave up counting.' Colin Gramp adds that he 'was amazed how many young men enjoyed it. Whether they were enjoying it to encourage the women to drink it also, I don't know. But it was amazing how it caught on'.

Above: Modern German winemaking technology was key to the development of the Barossa Pearl style in the 1950s

Reds under the bed: the other new taste of the 1950s

Meanwhile, a trickle of serious—and seriously good—red wine was emerging from the cellars of Woodleys, Hardys, Tulloch and Wynns. Some of these wines, such as the Woodleys 'Treasure Chest' series, developed by managing director Tony Nelson, an influential Viennese migrant, and the Wynns Michael Hermitage, would gain legendary status over time. But none would be quite as influential, or as controversial, as the red wines Max Schubert started making for Penfolds.

Gordon Colquist, long-serving employee of Penfolds, remembers how Schubert's first attempts at creating Grange were met with puzzlement and outright hostility:

[Max] came back [from Europe with] that [idea of making long-lived, new-oak matured red] and in 1948–49 decided to make this style of wine … Max had the different barrels. He found American oak was the best to mature it in … He made it and a few years later he showed it at the Beefsteak and Burgundy Club. The people said, 'Oh, that's a dry sweet wine.' It was really criticised. He battled up to 1958, when they decided that they weren't going to make any of this style that Max liked. He kept going, and in 1960 we had a person who came over from France and happened to stay with the management and they brought one of these bottles out. The Frenchman thought it was one of the number-one wines from France … He was quite enthusiastic about it.

Mrs Gladys Penfold Hyland was there at the time and Miss Longhurst, who was the secretary, also happened to be there. They asked Max if he could make it and show it. Gave him the full reins … They put it in the Adelaide Show and it got a gold medal and the best wine in the Show.

This shift in taste from an insular obsession with strong, sweet fortified wines to a more cosmopolitan appreciation of savoury oak-matured table wine mirrors a wider shift in Australian society that took place in the 1950s. Hotelier Oliver Shaul, a European migrant whose family had fled the Nazis, believed that the decade witnessed 'a march forward in all things. It wasn't just wine. It was food. It was the arts. It was painting. It was music … the whole development of Australia in all these things, some faster than others, was in tandem with the country opening up to other cultures'.

Another migrant, chef Hermann Schneider, arrived in Melbourne during the Olympic Games, and saw first-hand the change in cultural awareness:

[When I arrived] wherever you walked there were the same dishes served. That was very, very limiting in a certain way. And even the vegetables—there were firstly very few vegetables served … One of the first things that I did in the restaurant during my career [was to provide] dishes with vegetables that were complementary, on one side, and also which would be seasonal. And that was a mixed success. A lot of people would return the dishes and say, 'Look, take the garbage off and give me my steak, and my chips.' But, slowly, people started to appreciate it more and more and more. And a lot of people became interested.

From the vantage point of his family's vineyard in north-east Victoria, Bernie Gehrig's view was slightly different:

Whether it was the influx of Europeans after the war, or whether some of the Australians being in Europe at war time had a bit of dry red and then continued on that practice—I know that happened with a couple of friends of mine. Overall on a national scene, why the interest in wine just took off, I don't really know. I don't quite subscribe to the theory that it was the so-called new Australians. I think it was more that the Australians in general had a greater rise in their living status, rather than copying new Australians.

The swinging sixties: flagons of claret

Wine really took hold of the Australian palate and psyche in the 1960s. Between 1960 and 1970, per-capita consumption rose from 5.1 litres to 8.2 litres—with most of the growth coming from table and sparkling wine, not fortified. And it

Above: A flagon of Penfolds claret

wasn't necessarily the same people switching from sherry to 'champagne': much of the growth was accounted for by an entirely new, middle-class generation of drinkers. As Hunter Valley winemaker Jay Tulloch points out, fortified wine continued but it was 'the drink of the workingman', whereas the new rieslings, pearls and clarets attracted whole new sections of society to wine.

Recognising the changes and keen to make wine ever more accessible, the industry started looking for new ways to package and promote its products. Barossa Pearl's unusual but popular bottle shape and screwcap had shown that Australian drinkers were ready for innovation, and the wine companies were happy to oblige.

Wynns, for example, tapped the zeitgeist beautifully with the introduction of wine in 2 litre flagons in the early 1960s. Wynns general manager, Frank Devine, credits David Wynn with the idea:

Probably the most important thing that Wynns ever did was to start the flagon … It [gave] people the ability to buy a reasonable quantity of wine at a price that was affordable by most people … Although there were other flagons available, Wynns were the first to really market the product. The first ones that made it work. And it was basically in Victoria. New South Wales wouldn't touch it. And even in Adelaide, you could buy flagons but you could only buy them from a wine retail shop. The winemakers didn't go into flagons until well after Wynns got the thing working.

By the end of the 1960s, as Bob Hardy points out, this hugely popular new way of buying wine coincided with red wine becoming the drink of choice: 'The first great surge in table wines was reds. Everyone used to take along a flagon of claret. Every function you used to go to, they'd bring on flagons of claret.'

Suddenly, in the late 1960s, the pioneering red winemakers—O'Shea, Schubert, Preece and the rest—were joined by a new breed of boutique wine-makers, keen to make great, ageworthy Australian red wines like the classic, rare wines they had tasted as younger men. In the Hunter, Dr Max Lake was driven by memories of a 1930 Dalwood cabernet (drunk at the home of Melbourne wine merchant Doug Crittenden) to plant the Lake's Folly vineyard; in the Yarra Valley, Dr John Middleton was fuelled by a cellar full of old Seppelt burgundies to plant Mount Mary; in Bendigo, Stuart Anderson was inspired to plant Balgownie Estate by the great old Mount Pleasants he'd drunk at university. And suddenly, there was a thirsty market of wine-lovers eager to buy as many red wines as they could get their hands on.

Wine historian David Dunstan remembers that his family's first, tentative foray into wine in the early 1960s revolved, as it did for many other Australian families,

around buying fortified wines in bulk and bottling at home. But 'all that changed with the red wine boom [in the late 1960s], with the publication of Max Lake's *Classic Wines of Australia*,' said Dunstan. 'The red wine boom coincided with the minerals boom, with the new wealth of Australia. Home bottling came to an end. There were new plantings all across the country. It was a very exciting time.'

The 1970s: from flagons to casks, from claret to chablis

Ah, the cask. While Barossa Pearl and its ilk got people drinking sweet light table wine, and the flagon helped usher in a taste for accessible, well-priced red wine, the cask was the means by which table wine achieved mainstream popularity in Australia.

The cask—1 gallon (4.5 litre) bag-in-the-box wine—had first been developed and introduced by Angoves in 1965. Penfolds soon followed suit and introduced a similar product, although theirs was a bag of wine sealed inside a paint tin-sized metal container printed to look like a barrel. Neither company was able to maintain the success of these early casks, due to technical difficulties with the tap that dispensed the wine, and market perception. Wynns, on the other hand, overcame the technical problems, put their bag of wine inside a sturdy cardboard box, and soon became market leaders in cask wine sales. And once Wynns had shown it could be done, everyone else soon jumped on the cask wine bandwagon.

Says Guenter Prass of Orlando:

People have either forgotten or don't want to remember the huge influence the cask pack had on wine consumption … In the early 1970s [wine] consumption was 8.5 litres per head per annum. This increased to 21 litres per head per annum in 1985 to '86. No doubt the wine cask was the main contributor to this tremendous rise. The wine snob called it 'Chateau Cardboard', but the average consumer took to it. The ease of dispensing the wine, the ease of disposal of the empty package, the maintenance of the freshness in the ullaged container all added to its tremendous success.

Perry Gunner from Orlando believes that the accessibility of cask wines such as the hugely successful Coolabah range—with its immortal advertising tag line of 'Where do you hide your Coolabah?'—appealed to the Australian propensity for immoderate consumption:

[With] a cask of wine in the fridge, no-one actually quite knew how much you were drinking. You could go back and have a few more glasses, and instead of having to open a flagon that might oxidise before you got to drink it, here was a wine that was being preserved all the time during consumption. [Some people] even suggested that when Mum and Dad were away the children would go and help themselves to the cask of Coolabah in the fridge. So it became omnipresent, as we used to say, in households around Australia.

The surge in popularity of the cask coincided with a massive shift from red to white wine. 'Claret', 'hermitage' and 'burgundy' were sidelined for 'chablis', 'moselle' and 'white burgundy' (generic labelling was still the norm in the 1970s; a wholesale shift to varietal labelling—such as chardonnay or shiraz—was still a decade or more away).

The red wine boom had been huge at the beginning of the 1970s. Doug Crittenden remembers:

… a desperate shortage of red and people were hoarding it and putting it under their beds. They thought that they were all going to make a fortune out of it … I remember at one particular stage I bought some red wine that was made from [the aromatic white grape] frontignac and something else. I mean, you'd take anything that you could get that you could sell.

But the double whammy of a financial crisis and a health scare put the kybosh on red wine drinking. 'It collapsed like a pack of cards,' says Crittenden. 'There was a crash on the stock exchange … People had … thought that they could sell [their hoarded red wines] and they'd make money. 'Course, nobody bought any

[With] a cask of wine in the fridge, no-one actually quite knew how much you were drinking. You could go back and have a few more glasses.

PERRY GUNNER

Opposite: Royal Easter Show wine promotion, 1971

ENGLAND
UNITED STATES
MALAYA
JAPAN
CAN ORDER HERE NOW!
DIATE FREE DELIVERY
PENFOLDS
WINE

red for quite some time … So I mean it just went up like that and then crashed down like that.'

The health scare was triggered by an article that blamed the concentration of histamines in red wine for a number of allergic reactions in some consumers. The mythology surrounding this claim grew rapidly and sales of red wines died overnight. Bob Hardy recounts that 'this stupid scare came on about histamines in red wines … very, very quickly the swing went to whites and reds were almost forgotten'.

Bernie Gehrig remembers that in the early 1970s red was so popular that the Australian Wine Board ran advertising and promotions, exhorting people to try a white. And just a few years later, 'All we wanted to do was drink white, and copious amounts of dry red were tipped down the drain or sent to the still, or whatever.'

For Greg Trott, the shift to white was driven by improvements in winemaking technology: 'In about '76,' he says, 'the drinking habits of the nation changed. Because [we'd] been making white wine so much better and the climate obviously favours white wine, all of a sudden people were stripping reds right down and making white out of them because there was just none about and reds floundered.'

Despite the dominance of white wines in the mid to late 1970s, many new styles of red were also developed. Elegant, fine cabernets and shirazes from emerging new regions of Western Australia and the renascent Yarra Valley were beginning to get themselves noticed by winning high-profile trophies such as the Jimmy Watson at the Melbourne Wine Show. And up-and-coming winemakers, such as Wolf Blass, were thinking about how to make their red wines more appealing to this new generation of drinkers. 'I had to do something,' says Wolf. 'And my idea was to get women to drink wine.'

It had to be soft and smooth. At the time [Australian] red wines were so heavy. They didn't know how to make them. You put a spoon in, it didn't fall. The spoon still stayed in the red wine. And they were selling the wine by telling the retailer and the retailer told the consumer, you have to put the wine away, you wait for six, seven years and it's all right to drink. And I thought that was lunatic. So this is when this blending came in. The combination of different varieties, combination of different regions to make this wine drinkable, oak maturation to give them this complexity, and drinkability became the key word. And this is why I was probably successful. And I confused all of the judges! Because suddenly they thought that [blended wine] was the greatest thing since sliced bread was invented.

Australia's long-running wine shows, organised by agricultural societies in the capital cities and older regions such as Rutherglen, became more and more

It had to be soft and smooth. At the time [Australian] red wines were so heavy. They didn't know how to make them.
WOLF BLASS

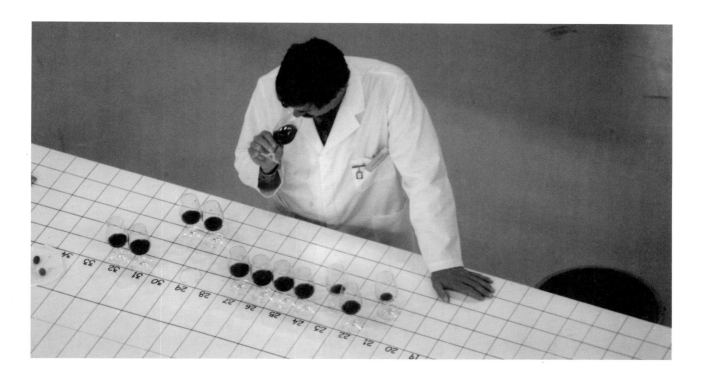

Above: Brian Croser judging at the Adelaide Wine Show, 1995

influential during this decade, moulding popular tastes. Not only did winning high-profile trophies such as the Jimmy Watson help to establish new brands in the marketplace, but the shows became a frenetic breeding ground for new talent and ideas.

'Take the Church Block blend,' says Greg Trott, referring to one of Wirra Wirra's most successful red wines. 'Cud Kay [of Amery] saw the first one I made in '72 and he said, "You put that in the show?" I said, "No." He said, "Well, I would if I were you. Any other show, stick it in. It's a fantastically good wine." Well, it set us up.'

Ivan Limb, who was a winemaker at Orlando, says the industry in the 1970s and 1980s was full of well-educated, competitive young people keeping an eye on each other's wines by attending the exhibitor's tastings at the shows. 'They were changing times,' says Ivan. 'In a funny way everything backtracked from the wine shows. Wine shows were very significant back then because they were setting a standard [and] you were trying to catch up with the guy winning the gold medal, and you wanted it.'

The 1980s: a rush to cool-climate wines

The industry was really picking up pace now, and drinkers were embracing the produce of the new boutique winemakers, as well as the newer, fashionable cool-climate styles produced by the established companies. Traditional warmer regions such as the Hunter and the Barossa were increasingly overlooked in favour of the new, different wines emerging from cooler regions such as Tasmania, the Mornington Peninsula, the Adelaide Hills and Great Southern in Western

Australia. These wines were made from different grapes, too: reds from pinot noir, whites from sauvignon blanc and chardonnay, sparkling wines made from pinot and chardonnay, and herbaceous styles of cabernet.

Hunter Valley winemaker Phil Ryan remembers the impact of this shift in wine drinkers' preferences:

The warm climate–cool climate issue was the big deal in the '80s … I think there was an atmosphere sometimes [in the Hunter] of being slightly threatened. [The idea that] now our wines were no longer accepted as being quality because they were not [from a] cool climate.

Winemaker Robin Moody's recollections of the attitudes at Wynns in the late 1970s and early 1980s are typical:

One of the things that stands out a lot was the change in Wynns Coonawarra Estate from grapes being picked on other parameters than just sheer fruit ripeness and flavour. John Wade had come from Wagga, and Brian Croser at the time was teaching pH and fruit flavour of a style that wasn't properly defined. Cabernet, in particular, has really strong characteristics at 11 and a half to 12 baume [the measure of sugar content in the grapes, which roughly equates to potential percentage of alcohol in the finished wine] and you can taste it in the field—especially at Coonawarra … We found in '79 and '80, when John was there first, [that] the wines were quite low in alcohol and quite green, hollow and, interestingly, quite spectacularly interesting as young wines, but wines that never matured into really good reds.

While these lean, green cabernets were all the rage (and before anyone had a chance to realise that they didn't age very well), and while the newer, cooler-climate regions were hogging the limelight, the big, ripe, solid red wines from the warmer climates fell almost completely out of favour. Alex Johnston from Pirramimma in McLaren Vale says that 1980 'was when we grafted 13 acres of lovely shiraz on lovely red loamy soil to riesling':

Because you couldn't sell shiraz. I can remember our Sydney agent saying, 'No, don't bother to send us any shiraz. You can't sell it here in Sydney.' A few years later, the South Australian government was paying growers to pull out vineyards because the regions' wines had become so unfashionable. But by 1987, the demand for pinot noir and chardonnay for sparkling wines such as the wildly successful Yellowglen had grown so fast that big areas of those two grapes were planted for Mildara.

The 1990s: full circle

As Australia cruised towards the end of the twentieth century, the wine industry was churning out a vast array of different styles—now all varietally labelled, thanks to the 1994 trade agreement with the EU banning the use of generic terms like claret and moselle. Tasmania emerged as a leading area for sparkling wines and great pinot noir; the warm-climate regions enjoyed increasing attention for their full-bodied shirazes once again and a new wave of spicy shiraz from cooler regions broadened the offering; cheap and cheerful chardonnay from the warm inland irrigated regions led the export charge towards the end of the decade; and winemakers started exploring a whole new world of possibilities in the form of alternative grape varieties such as viognier, sangiovese and nebbiolo.

Right at the end of the decade, powerful US wine critic Robert Parker 'discovered' the strong, dense, super-charged and alcoholic red wines being made by a handful of maverick producers in the Barossa and McLaren Vale—wines, in body, not unlike the 'ferruginous' burgundy and hermitage popular at the beginning of the century. Parker awarded these wines extraordinarily high scores—98, 99 even 100 points out of 100—and suddenly they were in fierce demand. Dot-com millionaires fought over these new, Parker-anointed treasures, prices went through the roof, and winemakers across Australia, especially in the warmer regions, started producing big, alcoholic wannabe reds, aimed squarely at Parker's palate.

During the 1990s, fortified wine sales declined at an alarming rate: despite having dominated Australia's wine market for most of the twentieth century, fortifieds were falling very rapidly out of fashion. Except the best ones. In the late 1990s, Robert Parker also went gaga over Australia's top muscats, tokays and ports, dishing out superlatives and more perfect scores. Again, demand for—and the prices of—wines such as Chambers Rare Muscat skyrocketed.

Bill Chambers applies his characteristically laconic philosophy to what happened after Parker 'discovered' his wines:

The whole [Australian] wine industry knew that Rutherglen made pretty good tokays and muscats but when somebody from overseas—not English, but somebody from America—says it, it's even better … We had to put the price of the old wines up tremendously—a supply and demand thing … And then you get a certain kudos when they're so bloody expensive. It's amazing, isn't it?

CHAPTER 2

IN THE VINEYARD

From horse-drawn ploughs to harvesting machines

If you go back to the basics—the soil, the climate, where we are in the world and the technology—we can produce the world's best wine. We've got a way to go before we get there but we've got the ingredients.

BRIAN CROSER

For the first half of the twentieth century, most of Australia's vineyards were farmed in virtually the same way vineyards had traditionally been farmed for hundreds, if not thousands, of years in the Old World.

All the planting, pruning and picking was done by hand; horses, not tractors, were used to cultivate the soil, to weed the ground under the vines, and to carry the harvest in; and vineyard work was a family affair, with traditions and techniques passed down through generations. In well-established regions such as the Hunter Valley and the Barossa, vines were seldom irrigated—irrigation was rudimentary in newer regions along the Murray and other inland rivers—and chemical use was restricted to copper and sulphur sprays to ward off mildews and other vine diseases. For all intents and purposes, Australian grapes were mostly grown using what we today would consider to be 'organic' viticultural techniques.

By the end of the twentieth century, just a few decades later, most of Australia's vineyards were being farmed in a radically different way. Almost everything, from planting to pruning to picking, had been mechanised; many large-scale vineyards were established by investment syndicates and multinational companies, and vineyard jobs were contracted out to highly trained graduates with degrees in viticulture; sophisticated, often computerised, drip irrigation had become the norm in all regions; and the use of synthetic chemical herbicide, fungicide, pesticide and fertiliser had become conventional practice.

Opposite: View of the Hunter Valley, New South Wales

THE HISTORY OF AUSTRALIAN WINE

The story of how Australia's vineyards changed throughout the century reflects the changes that took place in the wider wine industry.

Grape gardens and mixed farms

You can still find old grape growers in the Barossa, Clare and McLaren Vale in South Australia, as well as in other old regions like the Swan Valley in Western Australia, who describe their vineyards as 'gardens'. It's a legacy of the ancient practice of having vines growing alongside—even between—fruit trees and vegetables and chooks and livestock as part of a village smallholding, a legacy that dates back to the medieval feudal cultures of the countries that many of these old grape-growing families left in the nineteenth century.

At the beginning of the twentieth century, just after World War I, returning soldiers settled along the major inland rivers and planted mixed farms that included a few grapes. Roger Blake's father, who took up a 2 hectare block at Waikerie in South Australia's Riverland, was typical. Roger remembers:

It had about an acre of apricots and some nectarines and some peaches. A few oranges, a few sultanas, a few gordos [a white grape variety] and a few currants. The Waikerie Co-op was mainly a distillery at that stage. There weren't that many that had shares in the Co-op at the time, but my father was one of them. He used to dry his currants and his sultanas, but the gordos they used to send down to the Co-op for sweet wine.

Above: Harvesting by hand in the early twentieth century: 'a family affair … a whole town affair'

Glad Tinkler, whose family has farmed in the Hunter Valley since the mid-nineteenth century, paints a similar picture of her region in the 1920s:

When I think over it, there weren't many properties that didn't have a little vineyard on them … they would've had a farm and probably sold their cream to a factory … And they would rear calves and pigs and grow vegetables … A lot of them had this block of grapes. My grandfather did.

You can still glimpse that old Hunter mixed farm life at Tinklers' cellar door, where home-grown pumpkins, corn, berries and table grapes are displayed alongside the bottles of semillon and shiraz.

Around Adelaide, in McLaren Vale and in the Barossa, whole communities worked for big wineries such as Penfolds and Auldana during the week and worked their own farms in the evenings and at weekends.

Gordon Colquist's family had a small property at Greenock, in the Barossa, and he remembers the sense of community, especially around harvest time in the local vineyards:

We used to go and help pick, or put the buckets out ready to put the grapes in. Everybody worked there. It was more of a family affair, and a whole town affair. Everybody used to hop in together. It was a pretty close-knit family. It was still the bartering system there. We got a very low wage. If someone had fowls, and

somebody else grew vegetables, it was shared around. You just transferred over some of the produce to each other to get a better living.

While it sounds bucolic and charming to us in the twenty-first century, it was also backbreaking work at times.

Max Drayton's family farmed 20 hectares of semillon, shiraz, riesling and trebbiano in the Hunter in the early years of the century. The vine rows were planted 2.4 metres apart, wide enough to allow good access for the horses. 'The old hands,' says Max, 'believed a lot in cultivation.'

We used to plough in between the rows with a single furrow mould-board plough. You would go around the row twice with one horse, then we would cut the land in the middle out with a double furrow mould-board plough with two horses. For some reason we did that three times a year ...

If we got weeds in between those ploughings, we would hook two horses again on to a wooden harrow with spikes in it and we'd go up and down the row. When the weeds used to get too high to harrow, we'd plough again ...

The biggest problem with that [was that] the horse would stop as soon as he hit something pretty hard. If you hit a hard bit of paspalum [a kind of grass] he would stop. Then the biggest problem was getting the bugger to go again. So that's where the language came in. The language that he understood was swearing at him. You'd swear and he'd go. You could say, 'Get up, get up, get up.' No, he wouldn't get up. And you swore at him and he'd go. You know, some people had pretty vile language when they got frantic with him.

Then we used to go around with a chipping hoe and chip out what was missed under the row, which was pretty hard work. All labour intensive. No such thing as weed killers or anything like that.

The horse was a pretty smart animal. He'd know when it was getting towards half past eleven and you were heading towards the end of the row … so he'd go a bit quicker. And then you'd have trouble turning him around at the other end to go back. He'd sneak back the other end and as soon as you turned him around, he was off again. Because he wanted to knock off and he wanted a feed.

Norman Hanckel paints a particularly vivid picture of working the vineyards in the traditional way on his family's Barossa property:

The unique part was burning all the prunings at night-time with a horse going along in front and drawing the old burning wagon. All the cuttings were burnt … The cuttings were heaped in bundles along the vine rows, on every second row, and then the horse would drag this wagon in between the two, and then there'd be one person on both sides with a pitchfork throwing them in.

Hec Trevena's family farm and vineyard in the Hunter didn't see its first tractor until 1955; before then, Hec remembers delivering grapes to Elliott's winery in a horse dray. The crop had been harvested by hand into kerosene tins, and 'the pickers used to get a penny a kerosene tin. Eight and fourpence a day they'd get if they [filled] a hundred tins … Some pickers could pick a couple of hundred kerosene tins but the majority would pick well under a hundred'. With money scarce, they were glad to work for a penny a tin.

The 1950s and 1960s: modernisation begins

It was only a matter of time, of course, before the Australian wine industry was compelled to catch up with progress that had already taken place in the rest of the world.

As the Australian wine-drinking public's thirst for lighter, drier table wines began to grow, the industry responded by expanding into new areas such as Coonawarra and Padthaway; by introducing irrigation to regions where dry-grown vineyards had previously been the norm; and by modernising—and mechanising—the grape-growing practices. The ultimate aim was to grow larger crops of grapes, more profitably. As Peter Wall of Yalumba puts it, 'We were all in a bit of a scramble for grapes.'

The horse was a pretty smart animal. He'd know when it was getting towards half past eleven and you were heading towards the end of the row … so he'd go a bit quicker.
MAX DRAYTON

Right: Vintage time in the Wynns old vineyard at Modbury, 1920s

There were other reasons for the vineyard expansion. John Brown remembers that his family company established vineyards at Mystic Park on the Murray River after some destructive frosts ruined crops on their old Brown Brothers vineyards at Milawa. In South Australia, Tom Angove established a huge new irrigated vineyard, Nanya, at Renmark, to cater for the growing market.

There was a big change, too, in the grape varieties and even the clones of individual grape varieties that were being planted in these new vineyards. In the old days, vineyards were planted with cuttings taken in a fairly haphazard way from old vineyards—usually the most productive, healthiest plants. In the 1950s and 1960s, however, viticulturists began to import new clones of old varieties from Europe and California, and even new grape varieties that hadn't been seen in Australian vineyards before.

Tom Miller, then Chief Horticulturist of the Department of Agriculture, visited Europe in 1961, tasted wines in France made from the gewurztraminer grape, and realised that South Australia's wine industry was relying on a surprisingly small number of grapes, such as grenache, that weren't considered to be premium varieties in the same league as, say, pinot noir. 'We didn't have the variety

traminer … We didn't have chardonnay. We were living on varieties that were 100 years old and had been planted originally and no new variety introduced.'

At the time, however, strict rules prohibited the importation of new vine material: South Australia's vineyards were (and still are) blessedly free of the vine louse phylloxera, which devastated the French wine industry in the mid-nineteenth century, and still rears its ugly microscopic head in vineyards in Victoria. Tom remembers that, luckily:

… as it happened I was on the Phylloxera Board *and* I was the Chief Horticulturist, so I was in the box seat … the Phylloxera Act said [importing vines was] absolutely prohibited 'except phylloxera resistant varieties that may be brought in for research purposes'. Phylloxera resistant varieties … Now, it takes a long while to think about this. I looked through that and I must have read it a thousand times and suddenly saw that if we could remove the words 'phylloxera resistant', the Act then read 'except varieties that may be introduced for research purposes'. Governments are very difficult when you want to do something major, but very easy when you want to do something simple, and to remove two words from the

Above: A vintage festival grape picking competition in the Barossa Valley, 1949

Following pages: Vine pruning contest at Reynella, 1924

piece of legislation is nothing. I simply recommended that we remove the words 'phylloxera resistant' from the legislation. I am quite sure that nobody in the government knew exactly what this involved. And this was done. It didn't have to go through parliament, to do that you just have a proclamation.

Wine scientist Ray Beckwith believes that this decision to free up vine importation was hugely important in the development of South Australian vineyards, and Australian vineyards in general. According to Ray, this led to a 'surge in new plantings … gewurztraminer, pinot noir, gamay … Of those varieties, the pinot noir, perhaps, is the most important of them. But then followed such a stream of other varieties. Merlot and a whole string of them'.

The new vineyards in the 1950s and 1960s weren't just planted with imported selections, though. According to Tom Miller, smart vignerons such as Harry Tulloch were also carefully and seriously beginning to select and propagate 'varieties of red wines in the Clare/Barossa area on [their] own initiative. [Harry] had perceived that there were groups of vines in particular vineyards that he came to know well where they were better quality. He, if anything, was the initiator in Australia of [clonal] selection [where cuttings are taken for propagation from individual vines because they are particularly prolific or produce particularly good grapes].'

Not always plain sailing

Sometimes—often—it wasn't easy to convince conservative, traditional grape growers to change their time-worn ways.

Norman Hanckel started working under Colin Preece at Seppelt's Great Western in Victoria in 1948, when he was just nineteen. Norman had been educated in more modern viticultural methods at Roseworthy Agricultural College, and as soon as he arrived at Seppelt he realised that, despite being a highly respected winemaker, Preece 'didn't really have any idea of how to look after the vineyards'. He was, says Norman, particularly puzzled by the declining yields.

[But] he wouldn't let me go out and look at the pruners, and then after two months I went out and saw the people pruning. There was a gang of about forty and I wasn't allowed to say anything. I had to come back and fill Colin in about everything I saw. I said, 'I can understand—on the first day—why you're not getting any crops. They're pruning them incorrectly. They're leaving no fruiting wood and only rods that wouldn't have any bunches of grapes on at all. I'll go and tell them and show them.' He said, 'No, you do nothing.' And he tried to tell the foreman what to do, and the foreman said, 'No, how would he know?' Because I would've been nineteen then, I suppose. So finally Colin said, 'Okay.

Above: Under-vine cultivation by tractor at Wynns Coonawarra

They probably won't like it if you go out, but it's time that you went and showed them.' So I went out there and suggested that they go this way and the foreman took everyone [out]—they all went on strike … They all left. And Colin knew that would happen, unfortunately. I said, 'If I just prune it all right through the winter, you'll finish up with a bigger crop than what those guys will get altogether.' So he replied, 'Well, it's on your shoulders with Seppelt's—the bosses.' I told him, 'Okay, I'll carry it.' And that's what happened. So they all left and I went out pruning by myself and one by one I started employing new people and training [them]. Some of the old ones came back again. So that was all done properly again. They got a big crop that year.

Another Roseworthy-trained viticulturist, Neil Wilkinson, was hired by Orlando in 1963 to oversee their Barossa vineyards. 'Mr Fred Gramp drove me all around the properties and showed me what was happening,' remembers Neil:

It was a real challenge from where I'd come from in the irrigated districts and I found it quite difficult for a while … I didn't agree with a lot of the principles they were using in the old-style cultural practices but it was hard to get the old people of the Barossa thinking about new technologies and new methods. And that probably took a good ten years before things started to change. They referred to [the vineyard] as the garden. That was the thing.

In other, newer regions, a *lack* of strong, established viticultural traditions made planting new vineyards hard. Colin Kidd remembers arriving at the Lindemans property in Coonawarra in the 1950s:

It was fairly backward. There was no viticultural background … At places like the Barossa Valley, Clare, McLaren Vale, the Riverland, the whole community was involved in grapes. Down there at Coonawarra the community didn't think much of the vineyards at all. In fact, they used to talk about, 'Oh, well, in desperation if you can't get a job, you might get a job out in those vineyards' … And wire and all the things you needed to establish a vineyard were difficult to obtain. Labour was very difficult, and there were no family traditions. You couldn't get mums and aunts and uncles and all the cousins out pruning the vines in the winter time because they just weren't there. But we gradually built up. That was one of the reasons that we became very much to the forefront of mechanising viticulture in Australia. Viticulture changed from being very backward and staying in the past … with everything done as Grandfather used to do. But we couldn't do it that way. The companies wanted to expand.

Giving the gardens a drink: from dry-grown vines to irrigated viticulture

Today, virtually every vineyard in Australia is irrigated, using dam water, river water, bore water and reclaimed water. Drive through any wine region and you'll see black dripper lines running under almost every vine row, dispensing precious water, keeping the vines alive and fruitful. In the first few decades of the twentieth century, hardly any vineyards were irrigated, except in the warm, inland regions such as the Riverina and Sunraysia, where the mighty Murray and Murrumbidgee rivers allowed fruit—citrus, grapes—to be grown.

Bob Hollick of Mildara remembers these early days in Mildura:

Irrigation was a very simple matter. There were ditches. No such things as pipelines. You had a big channel running past your place on the edge of the road. There was a bit of a bulkhead there and the water would come across the road from a pipe and then into your ditch, which was just a dirt ditch. I suppose it was 3 feet [1 metre] wide and about 2 feet [60 centimetres] deep and that used to follow the contour of the land. The vines were planted according to the contour of the land in rows about 12 feet [3.7 metres] apart. The way that we irrigated was just to cut a wedge into the top of the channel, and we'd have bulkheads every

Viticulture changed from being very backward and staying in the past … with everything done as Grandfather used to do. But we couldn't do it that way. The companies wanted to expand.

COLIN KIDD

two or three chains to keep the water at the right level, and that water went down and flooded the rows.

It wasn't until the 1960s and 1970s—when, as Colin Kidd points out, the big companies wanted to increase production dramatically—that modern irrigation was introduced to 'premium' regions, such as the Barossa, that had traditionally relied on rain to produce a crop. Peter Wall at Yalumba was one of the first to apply lessons learned in large-scale irrigated wine regions along the Murray:

By the early '70s I, for one, was questioning whether or not the traditional practice in the Barossa Valley for viticulture was the best way to achieve a commercial outcome. We had the experience of irrigated vines in Yalumba's holdings up at Waikerie and quite a number of the others—Penfolds, Seppelt's—they all had irrigated vineyard holdings. So we knew the efficiencies and the yields of irrigated viticulture.

I recall that there was a horticultural conference in the Barossa Valley in 1972, and I was one of the speakers and spoke of the possibility of irrigating grape vines in the Barossa Valley. I suggested that I could see a time in the future when all the viticulture in the Barossa Valley would be irrigated. That had [some in the industry] in the paper the next Wednesday saying that this was an outrageous idea and we'll all be ruined. You know, the perception of irrigated fruit quality was that it was just no good at all. That was the environment when people were starting to look at irrigated viticulture.

In the Clare Valley around the same time, Jim Barry remembers installing drip irrigation at the new Taylor's vineyard—rather inconveniently, after they'd established the first 80 acres along contour lines, to allow for furrow irrigation. 'I heard about [growers] using drip irrigation in vegetables and strawberries in Toolangi in Victoria,' says Jim. 'And suddenly I heard that somebody was using it on vines. So I investigated it at the Department of Ag ... We changed then when the drip came in, so we had to plough through some of the rows of vines.'

Rise of the machines

One of the most significant developments in Australian viticulture during the second half of the twentieth century was the introduction of machine harvesting and pruning—both, again, a direct result of the big companies' desire to expand and find efficiencies and economies of scale.

Viticulturists from large companies such as Tolley, Scott and Tolley (TST), Penfolds and Orlando had witnessed machine harvesters being used in California's large-scale vineyards in the San Joaquin Valley in the mid 1960s. Mildara's viticulturist, Bob Hollick, was one of the first to trial this technology in the late 1960s, on a new 20 acre 'rhine riesling' vineyard between Irymple and Red Cliffs, near Mildura. The young vines had produced a lovely crop, remembers Bob, but:

… when I looked at them I thought that there's no way that we can hand-pick these grapes. I worked out that with the area of land that was under production I would need eighty hand pickers, four tractors and about three trucks to handle the harvest. I remember saying to Mr Haselgrove that there was a problem here. He said, 'Well, what are you going to do about it?' And I said, 'Well, the Americans are mechanically harvesting fruit. I'm going over there to have a look.'

So Bob travelled to the United States, studied the technology and, with the help of the CSIRO, introduced mechanical harvesters to the Murray Valley vineyards.

Meanwhile, Bob's young winemaker nephew, Ian Hollick, had started work at Mildara's Coonawarra vineyards. Inspired by his uncle's determination to mechanise the business of growing grapes, and spurred on by the lack of skilled labour in the region, Ian turned his attention to the laborious task of pruning the vines in winter:

Above: Mechanical harvester at work, vintage at Yalumba's Riverland vineyard, 1980

Myself and a lad who worked at Mildara, and is still there today, Brendan Provost, designed a machine that sat on the back of a tractor and ran off a 240 volt lighting plant. We had three electric hedge trimmers, and they were so hard to hold that we had to counterweight them because you couldn't stand on these things all day. But that was the original mechanical pruning done in Coonawarra. Wally Pilosio was a grape grower and harvesting contractor from Griffith, and I think he actually got the first grape harvester in Coonawarra. Bob and Mildara got the second one into the district. But Wally came back the following year [for pruning] with his circular saws mounted in a machine, and that's where the current circular saws took off from. Yes, they were interesting times because everybody was saying that vines would die and you'd never do it. But it was a case of have-to, really. And so, for the next few years, Mildara did a lot of trial winemaking, which proved beyond all reasonable doubt that mechanical pruning wouldn't downgrade quality, it was cost-effective and didn't kill vines. So we went on with that.

The 1980s: the viticulturists take control

If the 1970s was the era of practical viticulture and mechanical advances in grape-growing—from the introduction of overhead and drip irrigation to sophisticated clonal selection and mechanical harvesting—all advances aimed at improving efficiency and increasing yield, then the 1980s was the era of academic viticulture. New theories about climate and vine management were being developed and trialled, aimed at improving wine quality and, importantly, developing wine style.

At Roseworthy College, Richard Smart and Peter Dry's classification of wine-growing regions and development of new, radical ways to train and shape the vine's canopy of branches and leaves were pored over by vineyard owners, particularly in the newer, cooler-climate regions that had been established in Victoria, Tasmania and Western Australia.

Orlando viticulturist Neil Wilkinson says one of the biggest changes in the Barossa's vineyards in the 1980s was the move away from under-vine cultivation to an emphasis on not disturbing the soil:

More research and more knowledge became available with the various chemicals that could be used for under-vine weed spraying. There was more technology developed with drip irrigation and under-vine irrigation. The period of the '80s was really a major change in all cultural practices for vines, and to a great success. The less you can go into a vineyard with a machine that's going to cut around the soil, the better you are. These days there are lots of vineyards that don't get any physical cultivation at all. They'll be mown and they'll be sprayed for weeds, and that's it. And that's how it should be.

It wasn't always easy to introduce these methods, though. Ian Hollick remembers suggesting to his bosses that the company start using under-vine herbicides, and the very next week receiving from Ron Haselgrove a copy of *Silent Spring*, Rachel Carson's groundbreaking book on the disastrous effects of agricultural chemicals in American agriculture. 'I had to fight fairly hard to get those [herbicides],' says Ian.

But the industry-wide shift in focus from the winery to the vineyard was something that Phil Ryan, winemaker at McWilliam's Mount Pleasant winery in the Hunter, and others embraced:

When I first came here the winemaker was god and if you were given a choice of applying to do a course and you did the wine science course, you didn't do the viticultural courses. It was people like Brian Croser who turned that around and now viticulture is really the whole crux of the industry. Our understanding

I've always maintained that up until at least the '80s most winemakers thought that grapes grew in the back of trucks.

VIV THOMSON

of these special little bits of soil we have that produce these special wines, only because of where they are and what's happening within the vineyard, that's something we look to protect.

Viv Thomson of Best's Great Western also sees the change in emphasis away from wines to viticulture in the 1980s as a fundamentally good thing, and the basis for how the industry has developed in the ensuing decades. 'I used to go to the technical conferences and we would have 80 per cent wine, 20 per cent viticulture,' says Viv. 'It would've been about the mid '80s when we went to a conference in Adelaide and it was half-and-half … I've always maintained that up until at least the '80s most winemakers thought that grapes grew in the back of trucks.'

In recent years, this new respect for viticulture—for vine and soil health in particular—has inspired a new level of concern about the industry's environmental impact. Green issues such as carbon emissions reduction and wastewater recycling and composting are now commonplace topics of conversation. And in an increasing number of vineyards, winemakers are converting to organic farming practices, returning, as Margaret River veteran David Hohnen puts it, to 'Grandpa Farming'.

'There are some pretty daunting challenges out there, none of which is more important than respecting the environment and looking at how we can sustain the advantage we've delivered ourselves,' says Yalumba's Robert Hill Smith. 'But we can't do it with our eyes shut and we've got to respect water and land management and do something about it … because it's getting to the point that it's a real concern.'

Above: Viv Thomson

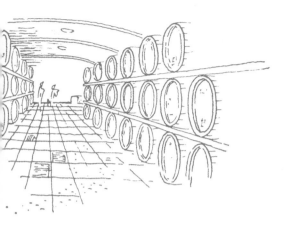

We applied techniques that were new, and we started making better-quality wines because of that.

JOHN VICKERY

You can experience for yourself what it was like to be a winemaker in the early twentieth century if you visit old wineries such as Tahbilk in central Victoria, Wendouree in South Australia's Clare Valley, or Tyrrell's in the Hunter Valley in New South Wales.

Each of these venerable places has left part of its winemaking area as it was 100 years ago: dirt floors grooved shiny with decades of wear; galvanised iron roofs held up by thick wooden beams; big old slate or concrete vats, vast oval wooden casks and creaky basket presses.

The big difference is, of course, that working in these places back then was a lot harder than it is today: there was often no electricity in smaller wineries, machinery was powered by steam and most activities were carried out by hand. Look at the photographs taken by Max Dupain in 1950 of cellar hands at Maurice O'Shea's dirt-floor galvo shed winery in the Hunter Valley, and you're confronted with the visceral punch of how bloody tough it was to make wine in those days and in those conditions.

The story of how Australian winemaking changed in the twentieth century is really one of finding ways to make the whole process easier and more efficient, to protect and enhance the fruit flavour of the grapes in often inhospitably hot conditions, and to ensure consistency of style for an increasingly discerning—and increasingly competitive—marketplace. It's also a story of how, again and again, Australian winemakers found the solutions overseas.

Opposite: Barrels of wine at Yalumba, c. 1962

A vintage snapshot: winemaking in the 1920s

Richard Haselgrove paints a vivid picture of how backbreaking it was to make wine in the early years of the twentieth century by telling the story of his father Ron's first vintage at Renmark when he was barely into his twenties:

[The] '21 vintage, I think it was … His task was to make 300 000 gallons of what was known as Sweet White NE 27[1] … Dad made this 300 000 gallons, he said, virtually by himself. He had no cooling, no means of fermentation control except to add spirit to knock some of the yeast on the head to slow down the fermentation. And then he had this unstable product. So when he got there, before vintage, here are all these dirty old concrete vats with wax and tartar and bugs. Every container was contaminated, and he had to try and get this cleaned up before vintage started. Anyway, he did it. It was quite a remarkable feat. But the people he had to help him were cellar hands who were prepared to follow orders but didn't really know what was going on.

In these early years, any technological intervention in the cellar was fairly rudimentary, often devised on the spot by resourceful winemakers rather than professional engineers. At McLaren Vale, for example, Cud Kay used to try to bring his fermentation temperature down by pumping cool well water through copper pipes running in two rows on the inside of the concrete tanks.

Things hadn't improved that much by the mid 1950s, when a young Norm Walker arrived at Wynns Coonawarra Estate:

It was all hard work down there. The [grapes] used to come in, in half-ton loads, in a horse and cart … [There was] no power there when I went down and we didn't have power when I left in '58. We had a steam engine. And the first job when Jock [Redman] and I used to get there at seven o'clock was to stoke up the old boiler, because you'd damp it down overnight so there were still hot coals there. Stoke her up and get the steam pressure up and then that would work the steam engine. There was shafting through the cellars and the only things that the shafting ran were a crusher … a must pump and the press. They all ran off the same shafting …

But the grapes came in and the side to the trays was only about a foot high … So they weren't squashed at all. They just came in as beautiful, full bunches. They'd fork them into the crusher and we'd put them in these fermenting tanks—open fermenters.

Unfortunately, some of the grapes that came in were better than others. Because they came in such small lots, you couldn't keep them separately. So they all went into a fermenting tank and the fermenting tanks weren't filled right up

Above: Colin Haselgrove inspecting grapes

because we didn't have refrigeration. The less you put in them, the less hot they got. So we only filled them up about halfway. They had strainers in the bottom—wooden strainers. You'd put about five or six tons in a fermenting tank. And then you'd add the yeast. I took up our champagne yeast [from Romalo Cellars, Magill] because that was as good as any for fermentation.

The [fermentations] were buggers to get started—to begin with—because it was always very cold at night. Then, as the vintage went on, the yeast would generate up and then they'd become too bloody hot …

We used to plunge three times a day—the skins would come to the top, so we had to keep pushing them down with plungers. Actually you'd walk around the wall—stand on the wall [of the fermenters] … and you'd just plunge them three times a day. Keep pushing the skins under.

There wasn't a lot of colour in the grapes up there because they were picked too early a lot of the time … And when they're not completely ripe, you haven't got the pigment in the skins. We had to work like hell to get the colour. And we'd leave them fermenting on the skins right until they went down to zero [until all the sugar had been fermented into alcohol] and then we'd run them off and put them away in vats.

You'd run the juice off—free run—and that went into your wine and then you'd toss the skins out with a fork into a wheelbarrow and wheel them along. That got tipped into the press—an old continuous press—which was on a different level. They were more like a mincing machine; they'd press the remaining juice out. We used to keep the pressings separate but they were never good enough to use for wine. They all went for distillation …

I used to like going down there to Coonawarra. Worked hard. You worked from seven o'clock in the morning up to about nine o'clock at night, I suppose, seven days a week, for about eight weeks … It was interesting because you really made the wines yourself. You got up and plunged them, you ran them off and you put them away and you topped them up. You weren't just giving orders.

But among this rudimentary winemaking—essentially unchanged since the Victorian era—technical innovations were beginning to emerge. Norm Walker's predecessor at Wynns was the Roseworthy-trained Ian Hickinbotham, who put relatively new theories into practice about controlling the secondary malolactic fermentation (whereby bacteria convert the harsh malic acid in grape juice to the softer lactic acid in wine). Hickinbotham had convinced owner David Wynn to let him make the 1952 vintage without adding sulphur dioxide to the wine after the primary fermentation (common practice at the time) in order to encourage malolactic fermentation. The experiment worked—the wine was softer, rounder,

more approachable—so, from 1953, Hickinbotham continued this technique. 'Those wines of Coonawarra Estate,' Ian remembers, 'were sold [at] less than two years of age. That had never been achieved in Australia before.'

Meanwhile, back in the Barossa ...

Ever since the earliest days of the wine industry in Australia, winemakers have had to cope with sometimes bloody hot summers. High ambient temperature is the last thing you want when you're fermenting or maturing wine: it can result in cooked flavours and increases the chance of spoilage. It wasn't until the 1950s, however, that efficient temperature control became widespread across the industry.

In 1946, Orlando's Colin Gramp had spent time travelling around observing the Californian wine industry and was appointed technical director of his family wine firm the following year. He was keen to implement the new temperature control technology he'd seen elsewhere in the world in order to create new styles of wine, so, in 1952, when Dr Brunke, a representative of a German firm, Munk and Schmitz, visited Australia to promote the new cold and pressure fermentation tanks for the control of fermentation, Colin leapt at the chance. Orlando and Yalumba both bought some of these tanks, but Orlando was the first to use them for their 1953 Barossa Riesling. The difference, says Colin, that the new technology brought to the flavour and taste was quite remarkable:

I always try and make the comparison that prior to 1953 the wine was open fermented. It therefore developed quite a bit of colour. It was then matured in wood, sometimes up to two or three years, and this lost its freshness. I think those wines were rightly called hocks. But with the pressure-fermented wine, particularly for the delicate rieslings from the pressure tank, after racking they'd go straight into a stainless-steel tank. So there was no likelihood of any oxidation ... When we were fermenting wine in these pressure tanks and being guided by the instructions, we were amazed how we could slow the fermentation down from normally three to four days in an open tank, to under controlled conditions ... ten to twelve days. As we eventually found out after fermentation was completed, these wines had much more character than the open-fermented ones. And there's no doubt about it, that slowing the fermentation down, holding the carbon dioxide on the surface for a longer period and particularly under pressure ... helped to retain the riesling character ... Several people used to call me 'Pressure Cooker Gramp'.

Ray Beckwith worked for many years at Penfolds as a wine chemist and remembers the 1950s as a great period for technological developments. Some—like

the move from crumbly old wooden vats to shiny stainless-steel vats to aid in the hygiene and temperature control of fermentation—might sound mundane to those of us who are less passionate about wine chemistry, but they were crucial to the finessing of wine quality, according to Ray:

The 1950s saw a big advance in equipment … We began to see steel tanks. These were the forerunner to the stainless steel. Mild steel tanks coated with a thermo-plastic resin. The vitrinite of the old Austral sheetmetal works. And they were very popular, and they were economical. Then, later on, stainless steel became very popular because the cost dropped from a pound [$2] a gallon—that was the cost of storage, about a pound a gallon—to about twenty, twenty-five cents … I remember Colin Gramp put in a Willmes press early on and invited us from far and wide to come and see the unit in operation. Colin was very generous in that way, of showing what he had. [And] with that advance in juice extraction, the table wines began to come into their own.

In the 1950s Ray also made contact with Dr JE McCartney, a world-renowned bacteriologist, and introduced sophisticated analytical tools such as phase

contrast microscopy, advanced microscope technology, to the winemaking lab at Penfolds. 'It makes the job so much easier in looking at what is in the wine,' says Ray. 'These things that we use, they're aids to winemaking. They don't make the wine but they help you to understand it.'

Bill Chambers of Rutherglen remembers feeling a sense of excitement, and a certain amount of pressure, as a result of all this innovation: 'Once the new wine-making came in,' he says, 'we had to be pretty smart to keep up with it.'

A tank on wheels: winemaking takes to the road

One of the technical—or, rather, logistical—innovations that would make the later boom in large-volume commercial table wines possible was the development of reliable interstate transport of grapes, juice and wine.

In 1950, an engineer at Penfolds' Magill winery called Frank Sheppard came up with a revolutionary idea:

Well, the winemakers were always complaining about the service they got to [transport] their wine to Melbourne and Sydney and Perth, and all these places were on rail. And just to go to Melbourne and back, a 1000 gallon tank [4550 litres] used to take twenty-two days. And they weren't insulated tanks, and in the summertime the wine used to get out of condition and they'd have to refilter it in Melbourne …

Frank suggested to Penfolds that they look into road transport but was told he was ahead of his time. So he took his idea to Samuel Wynn at Wynns:

I said to Sammy, 'Well, you're all grizzling about your service from the railways. It's not the railways' fault, it's your own fault. You should have your own tanker. You load it today and it would be in Melbourne in the morning, and the tanker back in Adelaide by midnight.' 'Oh, we can't do that. We've got no-one that can do that.' I said, 'You have. You've got someone who's going to have a go, and that's me.'

So Frank ordered a Foden truck from England, and had a special chassis built in Wagga. 'And then I made the stainless-steel tanks for transport. I did them myself. I built all my own tankers. All made out of ten gauge for strength, and it proved right.'

Frank's business boomed and inspired others, including Brian and Devron Booth, whose father had worked in transport with Penfolds, to establish their own wine transport business. Karl Seppelt remembers that it wasn't just finished wine that needed to be carted across the country.

Opposite: Wine in bottles leaving the Yalumba cellars, 1960s (top); delivering in bulk, 1968 (bottom)

We talked to [Frank] about this problem of hauling must around in tankers. Because in those days you had a hole in the top of your tank and nothing else. A couple of little valves, maybe, for carting wine. But you couldn't get the grapes out. So we got him to modify one of his tankers and put a great big valve in the back. About 18 inches round ... We had a little crusher up at Waikerie, and stainless-steel tank, which held about 20 000 litres. We'd ring him up, and say, 'Righto, she'll be full tonight. Come up and get it, and off down to the Barossa.' And at Chateau Tanunda we built our reception tank there with a worm in it. [The tanker] used to back up on that and we'd turn the valve on and away all the juice went. And that was the early days of fruit transport, which of course was developed [further] later on.

Thanks to Frank's lateral thinking and engineering ability, by the time the wine boom kicked off in the 1960s and 1970s, producers would think nothing of trucking grapes, juice and wine from one end of the country to the other.

The sixties start to swing

John Vickery forged his winemaking reputation in the early 1960s and 1970s, producing extraordinary examples of what was then the king of white wines in Australia: fine riesling. Indeed, some of the wines John made during that era at Chateau Leonay, which Lindemans had bought in 1961, still drink well today. For John, the key to what is still considered by many to be the classic Australian dry riesling style is very careful, cool, protective, antioxidative handling in the winery.

Certainly refrigeration made a big difference. Stainless steel [for storage]. Better hygiene. We were all [using] concrete tanks before. They were still in use and they were all fairly new concrete tanks but you still could get taints, particularly in white table wine ... We were using ascorbic acid and certainly, you know, gas blanketing [placing a layer of gas over the fermenting wine in the tank to prevent air contact], and gentle handling. Preventing air contact ... Centrifuges, of course ... So, clarification, refrigeration, better storage, probably a better understanding of winemaking too. Certainly microbiologically. We happened to be producing rieslings here and we applied techniques that were new, and we started making better-quality wines because of that. And that was technology that was really brought in by some pretty deep thinkers.

One of those deep thinkers was a Griffith-based winemaker called Ron Potter. Ron had the bright idea of enclosing a Ducellier pressure fermenter (bought second-hand from Jack Kilgour of Tatachilla in McLaren Vale) inside a normal,

Above: As the century progressed,
wineries grew larger and larger,
some resembling stainless steel
tank farms

large stainless-steel fermenting tank. 'The Ducellier unit drove an enclosed fermentation and used fermentation pressure to irrigate the cap [of grape skins formed on the surface of fermenting red wine],' says Ron. 'It was a combination of an enclosed fermenter and cap treatment.' The advantage of this invention was a reduction in the amount of sharp-smelling and sharp-tasting volatile acids in the wine, and a faster fermentation time.

The next thing was to get [a tank] that was self-emptying instead of having to shovel [the grape skins] out. That's what the Potter fermenters achieved—we put a 600 millimetre door on the bottom and we used to drop [the wine] through chutes into pumps, but that didn't work. Well, it did, but with frequent catastrophic results when the chutes tore off or something like that. Then we started putting them over bins—fixed bins and mobile bins. We built those and for years we built them around the world.

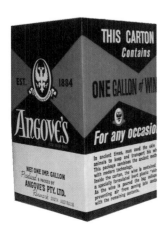

Above: It is hard to imagine wine being marketed like this today

Below and opposite: Tom Angove started a revolution when he developed the bag-in-the-box cask of wine; Bill Marshall from Angoves demonstrates the new technology

Not everyone was quite so enamoured of the new technology—especially when its introduction was inspired by the production of quantity rather than quality. Jay Tulloch remembers his family selling their old Hunter Valley wine business to Reed Consolidated in the late 1960s and watching as the new corporate owners built a large new winery:

I suppose, in retrospect, [there was] nothing wrong with building a new winery, but I think it's fair to say that no attention was paid to the technology that was being adopted, or [to] why the wines were what they were. Open fermenters and so forth were [seen] as all old hat. They went out the door. Ducellier fermenters—not Potters fermenters—came in. They did a good job, but I don't know that they quite produced the same wines and the longevity of some of the wines previously. Admittedly, you have to have change, but whether it was a bit over the top or not, I don't know. I think the focus was more on how can you cut down the labour.

Sometimes the new technology, while efficient, wasn't exactly cutting-edge. When he arrived to start his new job as a sparkling winemaker at Kaiser Stuhl in 1961, the young Wolf Blass was surprised to find pearl-style wines being produced with a second-hand aerated water filter from a soft drink company, second-hand

hermetically sealed retorts from a bankrupted local cannery, a separator on loan from Carlton United Brewery and a second-hand soft drink filling machine. He soon realised, though, that the man who'd put this equipment together, general manager Ian Hickinbotham, was a genius.

Today, nobody would believe you could build a fighting tank out of a sardine can. If he [Hickinbotham] was a German they would have given him and his engineers a first class Iron Cross of Honour. There was a spirit of achievement and excitement to get things done under adverse conditions.'

Wine to the people: the birth of the cask

Major innovations were underway, too, in how wine was packaged. In the early 1960s Wynns, Orlando, Leo Buring and others began selling wine in half-gallon (approximately 2 litre) flagons. The fortified wines stayed fresh after the flagons were opened but the increasingly popular table wines would oxidise over a few days in these larger bottles.

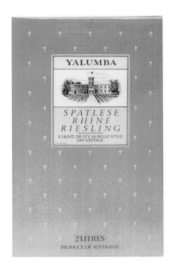

Above: Yalumba 2 litre cask range, released in 1984

Tom Angove responded to this challenge at his family winery in Renmark, in South Australia's Riverland. 'He was looking at a way of getting the volume of liquid to the marketplace cheaply,' says Tom's son, John Angove. 'That was the driving force.' Tom Angove's idea was 'bag-in-the-box' wine—what we now call cask wine—and the first, a 1 gallon (roughly 4.5 litre) cardboard container with a polythene liner, was sold by Angoves in 1965.

Tom 'certainly did develop that concept of the airless flow for a wine container', says John. 'He was the first and we had a patent for that. The concept of that original was to decant the wine out of the top of the box. You undid the top and you got the plastic bag out and you decanted it, and the plastic bag collapsed on the wine.'

While Tom Angove had started the ball rolling, his first attempt at the cask hadn't quite conquered the challenge of leakage and oxidation, and the product was withdrawn.

Ian Hickinbotham, then manager at Penfolds Melbourne office, was the next to have a crack at the cask by introducing a tap:

When I started at Penfolds I worked on the bag-in-the-box ... [A] man named [Charles] Malpas, who had been a First World War pilot ... [had] just developed his own tap. [Actually], I think I, as manager of Penfolds, developed seventeen taps with Malpas before realising it wasn't my job. Then I handed [the product] over to the technical division. I was horrified when they brought it out in a [container that looked like a] paint tin. All the bad connotations. And of course it leaked. I do blame the plastic suppliers. Nobody took it seriously. I found this has always been a problem. If you do something that's too new, you can't get taken seriously. Penfolds suddenly withdrew from it.

Wynns was the company that finally brought all the technical elements of the cask together in the right combination. Frank Devine was managing director of Wynns at the time:

The man who had [the first] idea was [Melbourne wine merchant] Dan Murphy, and the other was a man named Malpas, and he actually devised a tap that would work … At the same time, Penfolds started off with their round tin. Now, that was an excellent move and sold very well, but they couldn't get over the problem of leakages. The problem was, basically, the friction between the plastic bladder and the metal. And so they gave it up.

The marketing manager we had at that time was a man named Ray King. He used to report to me. I never claimed to be a marketing guru and Ray King put together a lot of the figures. So I went and found Malpas and I had quite a few discussions with Dan Murphy. By this time Ken Ward had come from Coonawarra to Nunawading and was very much involved in that. So we put together the wine cask and we put it in a cardboard box. And that got over the problem … And then of course, everyone else got on the bandwagon again. So the bulk wine, instead of being sold in the flagon, was now sold in what we called the wine cask. We didn't invent a flagon and we didn't invent the whole idea of the wine cask, but we did make the thing work.

Enter: the consultant

Much of the technological innovation and oenological nous (oenology being the part of horticulture that deals with viniculture) that swept through Australian cellars in the 1960s arrived in the form of migrant European winemakers, brought out to share their technical expertise. Some, such as Karl Stockhausen at Lindemans, stayed with their employers for many years. Some, such as a young Wolf Blass, fulfilled their contract and then branched out on their own as consultants and entrepreneurs.

Wolf Blass arrived in Australia in 1961 to work at Kaiser Stuhl, but by 1964 he'd set out his shingle as a consultant winemaker, beetling around South Australia in his old Volkswagen, dispensing advice to companies such as Woodleys, Normans, Basedow, Jim Barry and Bleasdale. As well as having strong opinions on wine style, particularly red wines softened by the liberal use of small oak maturation, Wolf established a model for the winemaker as charismatic celebrity. It was all very convivial and free-flowing, as Best's Great Western winemaker Viv Thomson remembers:

So the bulk wine, instead of being sold in the flagon, was now sold in what we called the wine cask. We didn't invent a flagon and we didn't invent the whole idea of the wine cask, but we did make the thing work.

FRANK DEVINE

Above: Brian Croser

I had a question on ion exchange, actually. And Wolf said to me, 'What are you doing tonight? Come around and we'll talk about it' … so I went around to see him that night. I think I arrived there at something like seven o'clock and we sat down and had a few drinks and had a meal … I think I arrived at seven and left about one or two in the morning. And of course, Wolf speaks like a machine gun. He gave me a winemaking lesson on just about everything you'd want to know and by the time I left that night my head was just about brain dead. Here was a bloke who was working as a professional consultant, who'd said come around and have a meal at my place and we'll talk about a few things, and he'd given me so much information just off the top of his head—I'd [only] met him that day. I've always had immense admiration for him because he was so … very happy to talk to you and impart [his] knowledge and help, and assist.

Winemaker John Glaetzer remembers an early encounter with the energetic young German consultant who would become his employer:

I'll never forget one day Wolfy lined up seventeen reds in this tiny little laboratory and said, 'Okay, Glaetzer, you pick out first, second and third.' This is basically before I'd tasted too much wine. Anyway, Wolfy wandered in probably after an hour and blew his stack because I was wasting time, taking too long. And I gave him my notes. You know, first because, second because, third because. And then the little German guy, his head hit the roof, he was jumping up and down, really cutting crook. 'You little bugger, you've been looking at my notes.' He was jumping up and down, and he reaches over to his back pocket and pulls out his own notes. In amazement he gets his notes out, and gets mine, and couldn't believe it. That settled it, once and for all. 'Glaetzer's going to be a winemaker and Glaetzer's going to work for me.' And that was it.

Brian Croser was another young winemaker who left the corporate life for a wide-ranging career educating, consulting and establishing his own wine company, Petaluma. Bob Hardy's description of the young Croser's influence when he was still at Hardys in the early 1970s captures the whirlwind energy, commitment to innovation, resolute conviction—and influence—of the celebrity winemaker:

Brian came back [from North America] with this cold fermentation, which had been pioneered by Gramps, but Brian came back and put it into practice for our company's point of view. Up until then we'd had very little refrigeration. And suddenly we had huge quantities of refrigeration and better facilities for making good wine. Actually, white wine sales had been very high before then, but the quality took a leap forward with that. That was the big change. I think the sales

were still very high but the quality took a great big leap forward. And that was just as well because we were being caught up with.

The rate at which the number of new vineyards and wineries expanded in the 1970s and 1980s meant that there was huge demand for consultants like Croser. Brian Barry's recollection of working as a consultant gives an idea of the spread of the ideas, expertise and influence of relatively few people across quite a wide cross-section of the industry:

I went into consulting with Brian Croser and Dr Tony Jordan. They had a little consulting firm called Oenotec, and so I joined them and did that for a while. The first brief I got was from a guy called Rod Scroop at Hazelmere. He wanted to make a small winery that would crush just a hundred ton and do very well. And we went to Melbourne for the wine show—Croser, Jordan and I—and on the way back we designed the winery … And we went ahead and did that and appointed a guy called Iain Riggs to be the winemaker … I started to consult to Wolf Blass … and to a guy called Wally Tonkin down at Currency Creek. And I was consulting back to my old firm Berri Winery. They gave me employment. They needed help, as it turned out. I was able to help Ian McKenzie. And I was consulting through Wolf to McGuigans in the Hunter.

The seventies and beyond

Phil Ryan sums up the attitude of the decade well: 'So, it was the Croserisms, if you like … it was the simple things [and] getting them right. You know, the SO2 [sulphur dioxide] correct and inert gas etcetera. So, all that was coming into the industry and people were more aware of looking for fruit flavour and retention. That was the '70s.'

Greg Trott of McLaren Vale winery Wirra Wirra agrees:

The '70s saw a revolution of a type in the processing of winemaking. Stainless steel came in, concrete and wax went out, refrigeration was another factor and the discovery that some pH levelling at the crusher in this area, which is a low pH area, by an addition of acid, was a huge benefit … I thought the '70s were largely to do with winemaking, wine science and the general processing of wines.

By the time the 1980s and 1990s rolled around, this clean, high-tech, protective method of winemaking had become entrenched as the 'Australian way', and a new generation of highly trained young grape-treaders were testing pH, lugging hoses, cleaning barrels and plunging caps in wineries from Pokolbin to Perth. Importantly, a number of those young winemakers also headed overseas to work vintage in Europe and elsewhere, often employed by UK supermarkets as 'flying winemakers', hired to drop into a run-down winery in, say, Romania, and apply some of that Australian oenological magic.

There was a certain arrogance about this: Australian winemakers had spent much of the twentieth century absorbing the best technical innovations from around the world, either directly, through travelling, or through migrant European winemakers. Now here they were, telling the rest of the world that they knew best. You could argue that this element of arrogance led in part to the complacency that settled across the industry during the boom times of the late 1990s and early 2000s.

Opposite: Yellow Tail's modern wine storage tanks

THE HISTORY OF AUSTRALIAN WINE

The biggest single contribution to Australia's success, I'm sure, has been education. I'm positive. And if we don't look after what we've got, that will be where we fail.

RON POTTER

In many ways, the spiritual home of the modern Australian wine industry is Roseworthy Agricultural College, 50 kilometres north of Adelaide.

Grape-growing and wine production short courses had been taught at the College since the 1890s but in the mid 1930s, two of the lecturers, Alan R Hickinbotham—affectionately dubbed 'Hick' by his students—and John L (Jock) Williams, started to develop a full-time, in-depth Diploma of Oenology course, with the first intake of students arriving at the college in 1936.[1]

Over the ensuing decades, the influence and reputation of this course grew to such an extent that the term 'Roseworthy' became shorthand for a distinctly Australian science-based, research-driven approach to viticulture and winemaking. Indeed, despite the fact that the oenology course (now, in the twenty-first century, tellingly described as a course in 'wine science and *business*') moved to the suburban Waite campus of the University of Adelaide in the 1990s, many people still refer to its graduates as being 'Roseworthy-trained' winemakers.

One of the first students back in the late 1930s was a young Ben Chaffey, who puts the initial success of Roseworthy down to the charismatic lecturers:

Alan Hickinbotham was the technical brains, if you like. He was the analytical chemist ... John Fornachon was a visiting microbiologist. He was an old student too, but he'd gone on to do postgraduate courses at Adelaide University. He was a wonderful tutor in microbiology. Then the one who taught us the principles

Opposite: Wine sensory evaluation in the 1960s

THE HISTORY OF AUSTRALIAN WINE

and practice of winemaking, who had been there for some time, was an old student—John Llewellyn Williams. So we not only had a neat little winery, which we ran under him, but we had wonderful lectures in viticulture, and in winemaking, and we had wonderful grounding in wine tasting. I suppose it's only natural I'd be saying this, but I think it was the best course that's ever been devised.

These early lecturers were giants in their field. John Fornachon's work into the bacterial spoilage of fortified wines, for example, transformed the commercial viability of the industry. 'John was a great man,' says Bryce Rankine, who ran the course in later years, 'both in stature [six feet four] and in reputation. He had a keen brain, great sense of humour, and was self-effacing with innate modesty. I was just so lucky to be able to work closely with him for so many years, as he was revered and became an icon in the industry.'

Another early student was Noel Burge, who remembers doing stints of practical work during each vintage he was at Roseworthy:

Hardys at McLaren Vale to start with … the following year, Emu at Morphett Vale … third time was Yalumba at Angaston. Then the fourth time—of course I was on the point of leaving Roseworthy—I came to Berri, and then I stayed there for twelve years.

Like many others who would leave Roseworthy and immediately launch themselves into a career as a cellar hand or winemaker, Noel says that those three vintage periods at McLaren Vale, Morphett Vale and Angaston were very useful in giving him hands-on practical experience.

Wine research: the early years

The same energy that led Hickinbotham and Williams to establish the oenology course at Roseworthy also inspired a whole generation of researchers. From the start, this research was aided by a strong sense of collaboration.

Ray Beckwith's story is typical—and also one of the most important. In 1932, young Ray started at Roseworthy on a research cadetship, in return for free board and ten shillings a week. Ray toiled away in the laboratory working on pure cultured yeasts—commonplace now in wineries across the world, but then a relatively new field of research. A couple of years later, John Williams presented a paper Ray had written on the topic to a wine conference in Melbourne, and the paper was then published in the November 1934 issue of the *Wine and Brewing Journal*. This changed Ray's career overnight: 'Leslie Penfold Hyland [of Penfolds] spotted [the article], and went in to my father and said, "Where's

Opposite: Advanced analytical technology such as the spectrophotometer (seen here in the 1970s, above) complemented traditional winemaking techniques such as maturation in large oak casks, seen here at Hamilton's winery (below)

that son of yours? I want him." So he contacted me and offered me the job at Nuriootpa. So I accepted that offer and started work in January 1935.'

The research Ray Beckwith subsequently undertook at Penfolds would have a huge impact on winemaking knowledge across the country and around the world. As well as continuing to work on cultured yeasts, Ray also delved further into Hickinbotham's studies at Roseworthy, exploring the role of pH in winemaking, especially as it related to acid additions. In his unpublished autobiography, *Keeping Good Wine Good*, Ray tells a story of being invited by Professor Macbeth from the University of Adelaide chemistry department to use their sophisticated equipment for his acid tests in 1936:

Professor Macbeth allowed me to use his personal laboratory for a couple of days. I worked away producing graphs of the effect of various acids on the pH of wine. [But] the professor took an interest in the work [and] I could not complete the graphs on two of the wines, as the professor had drunk the samples—those two graphs were completed with dotted lines … It was very remiss of me not to go 'armed' with sufficient wine for emergencies such as this, as wine is such good 'currency'.

The crucial finding of this research was located, as Ray writes, in the final paragraph of his paper, and was, he says, 'almost like a throwaway line: "pH may be a useful tool in the control of bacterial growth"'. This became the key to understanding how to stabilise wine through the addition of tartaric acid, now an almost universal practice across the industry. Ray's employer, Penfolds, led the way after the young scientist convinced the company to purchase a pH meter—a cutting-edge piece of winemaking kit that, back in the 1930s, cost the equivalent of twenty weeks' wages.

Roseworthy builds its reputation

Browse through the Roseworthy student list during the first few decades of the oenology course and you'll find the names of many men who went on to become legendary figures in Australian wine. Mick Morris, for example, now a grand old man of Rutherglen fortified wines, finished the course in 1951 with Ron Potter, the influential inventor of the eponymous fermentation tank. 'Roseworthy,' says Mick, 'was really the only course at that stage that taught winemaking and viticulture, because they had their own winery there and they had their own vineyard, so you got hands-on experience.'

[The course] covered all aspects of the wine industry. Beside the fortified wines there was still a fair bit of emphasis on the white wines and the red table wines,

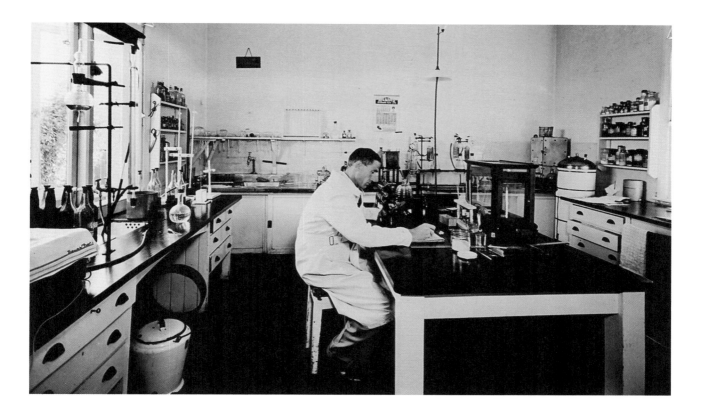

and we used to visit other wineries. I remember going to Leasingham, Seppelt, Orlando, Yalumba. We'd do tours around the wineries and have discussions with other winemakers … It was a very good background. You got a basic understanding of wine as you became involved in the winemaking. It was a great asset to have all that background and you got your own ideas as you went along, making the wine.

Another now-revered Rutherglen winemaker, Bill Chambers, started at Roseworthy in 1950 when he was sixteen, encouraged by his father, who had seen the benefits a Roseworthy education had bestowed on a Rutherglen neighbour, winemaker Dick Buller. Bill Chambers did the course with famous scions of old South Australian winemaking families such as Bob Hardy and Karl Seppelt, as well as John Vickery, who went on to make Australia's finest rieslings at Leo Buring's Chateau Leonay and Richmond Grove.

John believes that the collegiate conviviality engendered among a student body so saturated in inherited wine culture had as much influence on the future of the industry as the scientific training. In many ways, he says, it was a 'five-year holiday … We had a lot of fun'.

By the 1960s, Roseworthy had cemented its position as Australia's pre-eminent winemaking educational institution, and was attracting a growing number of students. Alan Hoey did the course in the 1960s and remembers a very practical side to his studies, in the form of monthly winery visits:

And when Roseworthy students visited a winery in those days—we were a group of nine—we were held in high regard as the future people coming into the wine industry and we were treated like kings. [At] Roseworthy alcohol was banned … I remember distinctly Peter Lehmann turning on the hospitality. After we'd visited Lehmanns we went down and had a barbecue—a long barbecue—at Vintners … I think we arrived back in the bus at about two o'clock in the morning from a winery visit. And it was there I got to know a lot of the people in the wine industry, but we were treated in a very special way. That practical side, particularly the winery visits, were very interesting and useful.

Kevin Pfeiffer, another student in the 1960s, recalls working from 8 a.m. until 5 p.m. forty-eight weeks of the year, and packing in many winery visits, to sit at the feet of the leading lights of winemaking and research. 'We … spoke with all the people like Rudi Kronberger, and the [Guenter] Prasses and the [Ray] Beckwiths of the world. That was the best practical training I think we ever had.'

Wine education spreads its wings: to Wagga Wagga and beyond

Demand for places in the Roseworthy course soon exceeded supply and, as the wine boom of the 1960s began to take hold, other educational options began to appear.

At first, these courses were small in scale and fairly ad hoc. 'In the 1960s, education became quite an important factor,' says Ray Beckwith. 'In the Barossa, Colin Gramp, with other winemakers—Rudi Kronberger and Noel Burge, myself, and others—formed a group in conjunction with John Chambers at the Gawler Adult Education Centre. We set up lectures at either Gawler or here at the Nuriootpa High School for the wine people.' The education program was quite successful, enabling some of the smaller producers to enter the field.

By the early 1970s, the industry was growing so fast and there was such great demand for qualified winemakers, it became clear that a new, proper course was needed. Ron Potter remembers being involved with a consultative committee for the College of Advanced Education—which later became Charles Sturt University—in Wagga Wagga in southern New South Wales when the idea of an oenology course was first floated.

At that time, interstate students couldn't get entry to Roseworthy … They only took students every second year. So that was very limiting. And the other thing was that there was no facility whatsoever for people in industry training and Wagga offered that. A prerequisite for entry was that you had to be employed in the industry. And the teaching was distance teaching. So that immediately brought a flood of support, and just in time, I think.

And when Roseworthy students visited a winery in those days—we were a group of nine—we were held in high regard as the future people coming into the wine industry and we were treated like kings.

ALAN HOEY

Ron says that the new project was 'blessed' by having Cliff Blake as Vice Chancellor: 'Once I floated up the idea to him of the wine science course, he picked it up. Nothing stops Cliff when he wants something.' Crucially, it was Cliff Blake's idea to recruit the young turk winemaker Brian Croser to head up the course.

Ron was sceptical. 'I didn't quite agree with the Croser selection because I didn't know [him]. He was only a young winemaker that had gone to America, as far as I was concerned.' But Croser soon made his mark at Wagga and began to influence the industry in as profound a way as Alan Hickinbotham and John Fornachon had done at Roseworthy forty years before.

Hunter winemaker Phil Ryan was in the first cohort of students to go through Wagga and remembers a feeling of excitement at being part of a new generation of wine education:

[Croser] had just left Hardys and his big passion was oxidation in white wines and making better white wines. He was determined to drag the industry up to the level that he'd achieved. And his understanding of the problems of oxidation, from a practical point of view, [was] just [a] revelation. It started a whole groundswell and I know there was a lot of resentment from the older members of our company, and other companies ... Brian was a pretty direct person, and

if he thought people were wrong, he'd tell them. He was very young. He was well ahead of his time … They were heady days, as about nine of us all started together as a group … It was that sort of little mob. We had a lot of fun. My wife used to reckon that I went away for a holiday every semester. [But] it was really hard work, those residential schools.

Back in the lab

The Australian Wine Research Institute (AWRI) was founded at the Waite campus of the University of Adelaide in 1955, funded by industry levies, and with John Famachon as its first scientific chief. One of the AWRI's early stars was a young CSIRO scientist called Bryce Rankine, who would go on to head the winemaking course at Roseworthy in the late 1970s and 1980s, further strengthening the connection between research and education.

The AWRI was founded, says Bryce, in response to the fundamental changes occurring in Australian wine at the time:

The wine industry recognised that its future lay in making good table wines, because in 1950 about 80 per cent of the wines were fortified [but] customer demand was not high. This transition to good table wines was thus crucial to the future of the industry, but presented many problems with which we became involved.

As well as obvious winemaking issues such as oxidation, hazes and deposits caused by trace amounts of iron and copper, and the need for better yeast strains, more effective use of sulphur dioxide, and pH control, Bryce says the AWRI was also involved in research into new grape varieties:

In 1950, vineyards were largely planted with grape varieties [for fortified wines] such as sultana, doradillo, palomino … These needed to be changed to the classical varieties of Europe, such as riesling, chardonnay, cabernet sauvignon, shiraz, merlot, pinot noir and the like … We worked closely with the industry on these and other problems, with the result that we were able to help effectively with the transition. Industry structure at that time was such that the level of knowledge was quite variable and in some cases poor, especially in the smaller wineries, so almost everything we found out helped someone.

In the late 1970s, when Prue Henschke returned from studying viticulture in Germany and joined the staff at Roseworthy College, she found an exhilarating enthusiasm for research being conducted by a small group of ambitious and talented people including Richard Smart, Peter Dry and Patrick Ireland, all of

Opposite: Quality control was an important part of the job for the winery's laboratory staff

whom would go on to become highly influential in the fields of viticulture and winemaking. Says Prue:

The exchange of information—new information—from Dick's angle after working on shaded canopies in America and Peter's work on pest control management, and then Patrick with his in-depth chemical knowledge, really meant that the whole idea about colour and flavour being an indicator for quality just blossomed from that little quarter. And I saw it happening. It was just amazing … It was the engine room … [For example] Richard set up the shade experiment. He wrapped some vines up in Norman's Gawler River vineyard and so we followed the grapes through to the wine and assessed the wine quality. Actually, it was done organoleptically. It was tasted by people. I remember Dick trying to get a lot of winemakers interested in it and in the end he got a fair crew of winemakers to come and look at this shading experiment. Because it was so obvious that the difference in quality between the shaded canopy and the exposed canopy, and it wasn't very exposed in those days, was just so enormous. And there was Patrick Ireland saying, 'Yep, this high pH, high acid, is due to the export of potassium into the grapes.' He had the chemical knowledge to actually explain what was happening. So out of that little trial, I think, a whole new area of viticultural experimentation came. And it was exciting. It was fantastic.

There were a number of attempts during the 1980s to further the connections between different groups, to consolidate the research for everyone's benefit. At the CSIRO, for example, Dr John Possingham was conducting viticultural research, but it mostly applied to table grape and dried grape production, which was, at the time, a much larger industry than wine grapes. Two delegates from the wine industry—Richard Haselgrove from the Wine and Brandy Producers Association and Bob Hollick from the Wine Grape Growers Association—approached the CSIRO with the suggestion that some of this work be channelled into wine-grapes, but they were told that the funds simply weren't available. So Richard went back to the wine industry associations, cap in hand:

I actually made an impassioned speech at an annual meeting—the council meeting—and put a case for the wine industry to put up money to encourage [the] CSIRO to continue work in vine research for winemaking. In the end what we managed to do was that the Wine and Brandy Association and the Australian Wine Board committed $60 000 of wine industry funds, in three years of $20 000 a year, and that money was put towards building the pilot winery at CSIRO Merbein [near Mildura, in northwest Victoria]. That then became a centre for viticultural research. John Possingham kept his side of the bargain and said that he would commit his funds in wine varieties. At the time I thought that was my greatest triumph, that I'd actually managed to get this very deep-pocketed industry, not keen to ever have money spent on anything that wasn't absolutely necessary, to put up the capital to establish the pilot winery there.

The success of this collaboration led to the establishment of the Australian Council of Viticulture. Richard Haselgrove was the foundation chairman, and chaired it for the five years of its existence. The Council, says Richard, had representation from all the state departments, from the CSIRO and, more importantly, from the two universities that had oenology courses, Adelaide and Charles Sturt. This group looked very carefully at where viticultural research in Australia should go, what was needed, and how the industry should go forward. 'Those papers are good reading still,' says Richard. 'They formed the sort of blueprint for what was hoped for from there.'

While the Australian Council of Viticulture didn't last, other bodies such as the AWRI and the Grape and Wine Research and Development Corporation, a statutory body founded in 1991, have continued to promote research and education. But, judging by the interviews conducted for this book, there can never be enough work done in, and never enough funds pumped into, these areas.

'Our survival as an industry is going to be through nothing else but education,' says Greg Trott, patriarch of Wirra Wirra in McLaren Vale. 'That sounds a bit sweeping, but I think it's vital.'

For legendary Rothbury Estate winemaker Gerry Sissingh, public education as well as industry education is crucial in order to ensure an 'open-minded wine-consuming population … [it is] important to keep on educating, otherwise we can lose them again. You've got to educate young people, let's say from fifteen onwards, that wine is part of your lifestyle'.

Above: Roseworthy College, 1970s

WOMEN AND WINE
Getting the balance right

The Australian wine industry was, for most of the twentieth century, a very blokey place. For proof of this you need look no further than the fact that a woman wasn't accepted into the oenology course at Roseworthy Agricultural College until 1973.

Women had always been a part of the wine workforce, of course, present in the vineyard, the cellar door and the boardroom. Indeed, the fortunes of family companies such as Yalumba, Hardys and Penfolds were influenced by some memorable matriarchs: the support of Gladys Penfold Hyland, for example, was crucial to the success of Max Schubert's new, experimental wine, Grange Hermitage, in the 1950s. But traditional positions of power—such as chief winemakers, wine show judges, industry politicians—were, until the 1970s, almost always held by men.

This old view of the role of women in the wine industry is illustrated by two stories, one from Bob Hollick and one from Bill Chambers.

During World War II, members of the Australian Women's Land Army were employed in vineyards across the country, including at Bob Hollick's father's place in Mildura. These young women were 'coming up to pick the grapes because there was no labour about and the fellows were still in uniform', remembers Bob.

[So my father] said to these two girls, 'Now there's the sultana patch down there, the dip tins are all out, you go and pick the grapes.' So the girls went down. Dad went down with a horse and dray to pick up what they'd picked at lunchtime and found about a dozen buckets filled with single berries. The poor girls! My dad was at fault because he just didn't bother to go and show them what to do. They'd go to a bunch of grapes and pick the berries off one by one [rather than picking the whole bunch as normal] and drop them into the dip tins. Oh dear!

For a long time, during the middle years of the century, Bill Chambers' mother ran the cellar door and mail order business at their Rutherglen winery: '[But] she was brought up in a true Presbyterian tradition. Somebody was ordering a fair bit of wine in bulk and she [replied to them], "I won't send you any wine this time because I think you're drinking too much". The customer kept the letter and treasured it.'

Australian society heaved itself through enormous social change in the 1960s and 1970s, and so too did the Australian wine industry. But, remarkably, when the first female student, Pam Dunsford, was accepted into the winemaking course at Roseworthy it caused a real fuss. 'In those days,' remembers Bruce Redman, 'Roseworthy was still a bit of an anachronism. It was still an all-male college, up until Pam came in 1973, and it was ruled almost like what was my impression of an English boarding school.'

'I started to drink red wine at uni and then became really interested in it,' says Pam. 'When I was doing second-year Ag Science, people like Brian Croser, Geoff Weaver [both of whom also went on to become winemakers] were doing fourth year [on

the oenology course] … There were a lot of wine-interested people [and] I just decided that I wanted to study winemaking.'

At the time, Roseworthy was an agricultural college, answerable to Tom Casey, the Minister of Agriculture in South Australia. But change was afoot: members of the Roseworthy board included some of the professors at the Waite Institute in Adelaide, where Pam was studying, who were actively trying to get women into Roseworthy. 'At the same time,' says Pam:

Malcolm Fraser was making all of the educational institutions autonomous. That meant that Roseworthy could no longer be an all-male college. And so even though the principal at the time, [Bob] Herriot, didn't want to have women—very strongly didn't want to have women in the school—because I had a degree and all the related subjects, he just couldn't not let me enter. And there were these other persuasive elements

coming from the Waite, and I think even [from] Tom Casey, to say that you'd better let a woman in … So [there I was with] 180 post-pubescent boys and I was twenty-two … they put me in [what had been] the infectious diseases ward. That was logical because it was the only place that had its own lavatory facilities and bathroom, but it's also probably a little bit indicative of the attitude.

Roseworthy accepting its first female winemaking student was a breakthrough for gender equality in academia, but the wine industry itself was still resistant to change. After she graduated, Pam had trouble finding work—until she approached Glenloth winery's Morgan Yeatman, who was looking for someone to replace winemaker Alan Hoey. Morgan remembers:

Left (above): Vanya Cullen, one of Australia's most respected winemakers and wine show judges

Left (below): Miss Australia 1966, Tania Verstak, Mrs Whyndam Hill Smith and Mrs Mark Hill Smith

Opposite (above): Pam Dumsford leads a team of judges at the Adelaide Wine Show, 1995

Opposite (below): Prue Henschke

to help someone do something, or get into it, you've got the job.' She said that, yes, she was. That was the best move that ever happened because that was Pam Dunsford. I was the first bloke to take on a female.

Pam Dunsford's Roseworthy experience encouraged other women to enter the industry in roles traditionally held by men. Di Davidson, who went on to become one of Australia's leading viticulturists, started her career at Penfolds in 1975 and soon encountered some entrenched attitudes among her male colleagues.

Armed with a degree in biochemistry, Di had answered an advertisement for a wine chemist's assistant—and was promptly offered the job of national vineyards manager by Jeffrey Penfold Hyland himself.

What they really needed, and they knew they needed it, was knowledge on soil and water management, which I could bring … [But] when I started the job I was twenty-eight, single and with a university degree. And the five people who reported to me— the five vineyard managers in Coonawarra, Barossa, Modbury in those days and Magill, and the Riverland—they were all of an age such that they'd been with the company for more than thirty years. They were nearly all in their fifties. And to be confronted with me was not easy for them. I really had to devise very quickly a means of reassuring them that I certainly didn't want their jobs and that if we could work

She'd been refused positions with two other wineries because she was a girl. She had a Bachelor of Agricultural Science. And I remember interviewing her, and I said, 'If you are willing to climb ladders and look and listen and pull a hose if it's necessary

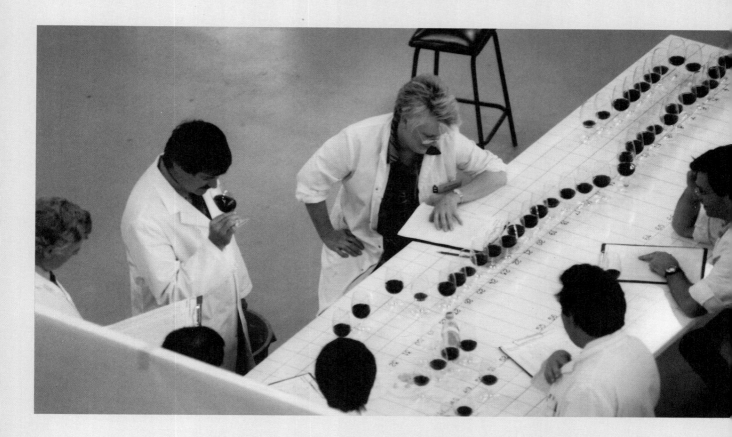

together, not only would their jobs be easier and better, but the results would be better. I learned to sow the seed of an idea and wait for it to germinate and [then] come back to me as their idea.

Because Penfolds at the time was family-owned, it was relatively easy to make groundbreaking decisions like hiring Australia's first female vineyard manager. But within a couple of years, the company had fallen under corporate ownership, first by Tooth's brewery, then Adsteam, and attitudes changed. While she says she was taken seriously by senior management, Di soon left Penfolds. 'I didn't feel comfortable in what was then the Adsteam corporate environment,' she says. 'I couldn't see women, in particular—maybe because there was so few women then—being given a management role in a time frame that I would've enjoyed.'

By the end of the 1970s, Pam Dunsford and Di Davidson weren't the only women working in high-profile positions in the wine industry. Prue Henschke had joined the research team at Roseworthy; Di Cullen in Margaret River, and other new vignerons were setting a fantastic example as boutique wine pioneers. The image of Australia's wine industry as being a big, boozy gentlemen's club had changed forever.

CHAPTER 5

MIGRANTS AND MAGPIES

The international influence

In the middle '50s and early '60s Australia imported winemakers from overseas to introduce new winemaking techniques for table wines. Today Australian winemakers are engaged overseas to preach the gospel and to introduce Australian winemaking practices … [That's] a remarkable change.

GUENTER PRASS

One of the reasons Australian wines became enormously popular around the world in the late 1980s and the 1990s was because they tasted so *different*. Many people in the UK and the United States didn't even know Australia *made* wine, let alone wine so vibrant, fruity, clearly labelled and user-friendly. Here was delicious novelty in a bottle. Many wine drinkers, discovering Australia for the first time, felt like these sun-kissed chardonnays and shirazes had sprung from nowhere, overnight. These were wines that emphatically, proudly expressed their New World provenance.

The reality was that winemakers Down Under had been influenced by the Old World for well over 100 years. Without the steady cross-flow of information, inspiration and innovation between the northern and southern hemispheres, Australian wines might never have seduced the world in the 1980s and 1990s.

Throughout the twentieth century, Australian winemakers made pilgrimages to classic and emerging regions around the globe—to France, the high temple of fine wine; to Germany; to California—to taste and study and see how things were done. They embarked on technical trips: winemakers wanted to learn how to fix specific problems and study at international wine schools. They went on fact-finding missions, ferreting around in cellars and wineries, looking for new techniques to emulate. They indulged in 'benchmarking exercises': if you wanted to make pinot noir in Australia, it made sense to visit Burgundy, the home of pinot noir. And they travelled for business: Australian winemakers were hired to

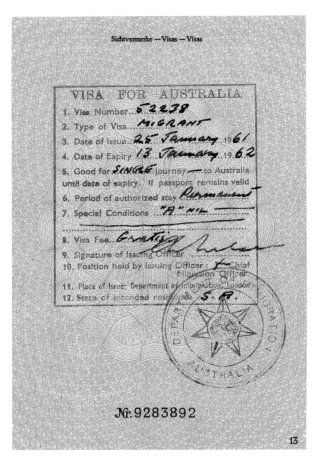

Above: Wolf Blass and his visa for Australia, 1961

make wine overseas, and wine companies invested in the international industry by setting up joint ventures or buying other wineries.

Meanwhile, winemakers in Europe, the United States and elsewhere looked on curiously as their counterparts in this strange, hot country on the other side of the world pioneered new regions, built new wineries, and forged their own unique winemaking culture. And, wondering what could be learned from Australia, many Europeans, Americans and South Africans visited, looking for inspiration and knowledge. Some even liked it so much they moved here to live, and became hugely important in developing the industry.

This ongoing cross-pollination of ideas has its critics. Some believe that because roving Australian winemakers freely disseminated their sunshine-in-a-glass techniques in the early 1990s, many other New World wine countries such as Chile and Argentina are now producing the very oceans of well-made, competitively priced wine that threaten to flush Australia out of the international marketplace. Then again, it works both ways: young Australian winemakers are still travelling, more than ever, regularly working vintage with progressive, dynamic producers around the globe, and they're returning with a desire to make an ever more diverse range of wine styles back home. This can only be a good thing for Australian wine lovers.

Yalumba's Peter Wall sums up the debt that Australia, the quintessential New World wine country, owes to the Old World:

We have been enormously lucky with the response we've had out of Europe. In my foraging around Europe to get new clones and new varieties, you need but ask … There's always been some antipathy between the Europeans and the Australians in … negotiations over trade access to their markets, or whatever it's been. But at the practical level, when you get past that and get down to dealing with winemakers or viticulturists, they have been extraordinarily generous.

The migrants

The story of Australian wine began, of course, with migrants. Spindly European vine cuttings arrived with the First Fleet in 1788, and subsequent waves of early settlers brought more and more of their wine culture with them. In the nineteenth century, whole communities uprooted from Europe replanted themselves in wine regions across the country: Lutherans, fleeing persecution in Silesia, formed the cultural foundations of the Barossa in the 1840s; families of trained Swiss 'vine-dressers' helped create grand wine estates in the Yarra Valley and Geelong in the 1850s; and in Rutherglen in the 1860s and 1870s, the needs of the thirsty gold miners were met by the produce of new vineyards established by English and Scottish families such as the Morrises, Chambers, Smiths and Campbells.

In the Swan Valley, on the outskirts of Perth, many vineyards were established by Croatian settlers after World War I—hence the presence today of winemakers with names like Kosovich and Talijancich. In 1924 one of these migrants was 16-year-old Joe Zekulich, whose family back in Croatia used to make a little wine as part of a mixed farm that also grew tobacco and 'anything for living … all kind of food'. Joe's story could have been told by many others:

Well, after the First World War, the problem was then that the Russian revolution was on. And when the communists win the war, 75 000 officers crossed from Russia to Yugoslavia. King Alexander, at the time, give them every job that's possible … [They started] learning grafting vines and all that … So my father said to me, 'Son—vineyards were burnt during the war … [It] will take us a long time to repair it and you've got no chance here. The best thing would be to go to America' … And then English Consul just say that Australia's a good country to go. That there you earn a pound a day. [In Croatia] I work three or four weeks for one pound. So I work in the vineyard and wine cellar forty-one days to buy a pair of shoes … There was several of us coming to Australia at the time. Actually, I was youngest out of whole lot.

After working in cellars and vineyards belonging to other members of the Croatian community, Joe eventually settled in the Swan Valley and established his own vineyard. Visit the Swan Valley today and you can still glimpse some of that old Croatian mixed-farm culture in the form of vines trained up on pergolas over backyards, where vegie patches grow 'all kind of food', and chooks scratch around in the red dirt.

Following World War II, another wave of migration would have a huge impact on Australian wine. The burgeoning Italian communities in Melbourne and Adelaide gratefully soaked up the trickle of table wines—particularly reds—produced in the 1940s and 1950s, when Anglo Aussies were still fixated on fortifieds.

Alec Baxendale owned a 70 acre vineyard in McLaren Vale during the 1940s and 1950s, and often had trouble selling his grapes because there simply wasn't enough demand for table wines. Except from the Italians: 'I had shiraz left on the vines here a couple of years, and also grenache. But the grenache were all right to get rid of because a lot of Italians had come from the Adelaide area down south to buy wine grapes for backyard winemaking.'

Around the same time, winemaker John Brown would regularly travel by train from Milawa in Victoria's north-east with hogsheads full of dry red for home-bottlers in the Italian community in Carlton in the 1950s, as well as supplying the local Italian tobacco growers back in the King Valley. Many of those tobacco-farming families, such as the Pizzinis and the Dal Zottos, are now among the north-east's top grape growers and winemakers.

German winemakers also had a great influence on Australian wine in the 1950s and early 1960s. In 1952, when Dr Brunke from the German firm of Munk and Schmitz visited the Barossa, he impressed Orlando and Yalumba with the new pressure fermentation tanks his firm was producing. To help them get the most from this new technology, Orlando advertised for a winemaker in German wine magazines. A 29-year-old wine technician named Guenter Prass applied for—and got—the job.

I went to my boss [in Germany] and said that I would like to have three years of unpaid leave. And he said, 'What are you going to do?' I replied, 'Go to Australia.' And he said, 'Australia? What are you going to do there? There are only black people and kangaroos. Are you going to become a hunter?' I told him, 'No. There's supposedly a wine industry there.' And I showed him the advertisement. So, after some discussion, he said, 'Okay, you can go for three years' … And that was the start.

The white wines Prass helped to create at Orlando, and the wines being made by other migrant winemakers such as Dutchman Gerry Sissingh and German Karl Stockhausen at Lindemans in the early 1960s, were among the first to really define the clean, fruit-driven, fresh, fault-free style we now think of as distinctively Australian.

The development of the wine industry in Western Australia benefited from American visitors. In 1955, Harold Olmo, professor of viticulture from the University of California, Davis, travelled through the state's south-west, and wondered aloud why grapes—well established by that point in the hot Swan Valley—were not being grown in places like Mount Barker, which were much more suited to producing finer, more elegant styles of wine. Olmo's vision reinforced observations that had been made by the legendary Houghton winemaker Jack Mann, and Western Australian viticulturist Bill Jamieson, and led to the establishment of the Great Southern wine region.

Another renowned Californian, Robert Mondavi, travelled to Margaret River in the early 1970s, looking to invest in the up-and-coming region. At that time, California was one of the most exciting New World wine districts, full of the experimentation, innovation and enthusiasm beginning to seep across Australia. Although Mondavi didn't end up investing in the region, he did encourage two of Margaret River's more ambitious new vignerons, Denis and Tricia Horgan at Leeuwin Estate, by introducing them to the benchmark wines from France—literally, by opening bottles. Tricia Horgan remembers Mondavi holding forth over countless bottles of white burgundy at the kitchen table:

Mondavi would say, 'I think that this property can produce chardonnays that rival these [the world's greatest wines].' And I'd look at the three-quarters-full bottles at the end of the tasting and think, 'What am I going to cook with these?' I couldn't bear to throw them out … We had one of the great men of wine in the world that was our mentor, and had made us focus on quality … I often say about Margaret River, that they owe a lot to those people. Because the founding fathers of Margaret River didn't go there to make money out of wine, they went there to produce great wines—wines that they could be proud of. And it was a by-product of that if they made any money. And they set the standards that have made Margaret River what it is today; because those that followed them had that to aspire to.

The magpies

Now, in the early twenty-first century, whenever a young, wide-eyed winemaker jets off from Sydney or Melbourne to Europe to travel through the winelands, do vintage in Spain or France, or visit the great wine estates, he or she is travelling in the footsteps of many Australian winemakers who have gone before.

I went to my boss [in Germany] and said that I would like to have three years of unpaid leave. And he said, 'What are you going to do?' I replied, 'Go to Australia.' And he said, 'Australia? What are you going to do there?'

GUENTER PRASS

Thomas Hardy, who established his eponymous wine company in Adelaide in the 1850s, travelled extensively in California in the late nineteenth century, picking up tips and pointers from that state's young wine industry. A young Maurice O'Shea was sent to study in France during World War I, and ended up lecturing on wine chemistry at the University of Montpellier before returning to establish his rudimentary Mount Pleasant winery in the Hunter, where he became one of Australia's legendary winemakers in the 1930s and 1940s, using techniques and knowledge he'd picked up in Europe.

And in 1923 a young South Australian, Ron Haselgrove, persuaded his father to pay his fare to France, where he worked in Cognac and Bordeaux, met up with the Cruse family of Château Pontet-Canet, and studied, as O'Shea had done, at Montpellier. Ron's son, Richard, believes this European experience was invaluable. On Ron's return to Australia, he was offered a job by 'Skipper' Angove in Renmark:

… and so he moved up there as a young winemaker … [where] his skill that he'd picked up in Cognac on brandy distilling was put to use … Ron didn't have the paper qualifications but was probably as knowledgeable a chemist and a scientist in wine as anyone in Australia. There were very few qualified people. Most of the winemaking fraternity were qualified in medicine or another field. Very few had actually studied oenology as such.

During the second half of the century, Penfolds developed a tradition of sending their winemakers and wine chemists overseas to learn about the latest technology and innovations, and pick up new winemaking techniques. The first and most famous of these travellers, of course, was Max Schubert, whose trip to Europe in 1950—ostensibly to find out how to make better sherry in Spain—inspired the creation of Australia's most famous red wine, Penfolds Grange. Gordon Whitrod worked in Penfolds' cellars at Magill at the time and was impressed when Schubert brought back stories of tasting young, partially barrel-fermented red Bordeaux in the cellars of Christian Cruse:

[The French] took him to heart because Max was a very good talker, very diplomatic, and they showed him through the cellars—what they used to do and how they used to make the wine. Max said, 'This is a wine for the future. This is something that we have to do in Australia.'

In the early 1960s, the place to go was America. As well as the University of California, Davis, which was building a worldwide reputation for its oenology course, progressive Californian winemakers had planted new clones of classic

grape varieties such as pinot noir, chardonnay, cabernet and merlot—most of
which were barely known in Australia at this time—and were making some very
impressive wines. 'It was pretty obvious,' says Karl Seppelt, who studied at Davis
in the 1960s, 'after being through Europe and everywhere else, that if we wanted
to get into the table wine business in a big way, which most people weren't [doing]
in those days, we should start to try and import some of these better clones.'

David Tolley was inspired to pioneer new grapes in the Barossa during one
of 'a number of trips overseas' in the early 1970s. Stumbling across a small cellar
door in Alsace, he and his wife Elizabeth encountered wines made from gewurztraminer and sylvaner, grapes they'd not heard of before.

We tried [them] and we thought [they were] marvellous. So, on my return to
Adelaide, I said to my brothers, 'We tried this very nice wine, gewurztraminer,
and sylvaner'. 'Oh,' they said, 'we're not that interested really but give it a go.'
I was able to procure three cuttings of this gewurztraminer. And three cuttings
of sylvaner, and three cuttings of pinot noir—the varieties that we didn't have in
the Barossa in those days … [By] the following year I think I had about thirty
cuttings, and I planted those in the Barossa. And that was the beginning of our
gewurztraminer. And we did very well with that variety in Australia.

Stephen and Prue Henschke studied winemaking and viticulture at the Geisenheim Wine Institute in Germany in the mid 1970s. 'There's a lot that I've retained from that time,' remembers Stephen. He acknowledges the huge influence Geisenheim had on his white wine making. 'The Germans are real perfectionists, so I learned this perfectionist attitude in terms of winemaking … [At the time] our whites were much more phenolic, broader, heavier, high-alcohol wines without the same finesse and fruit. So I really wanted to introduce better equipment, better technology, for improving the white wines.'

By the late 1970s and early 1980s, the Australian winemakers started to feel a lot more confident, and began to acquire wineries and establish vineyards overseas. Len Evans dreamed up a particularly grandiose vision when, after securing the backing of a financier, Peter Fox, and the winemaking talents of the young Brian Croser, he purchased property in California and a chateau in France. Peter Fox's death in 1981 forced Evans to sell the estates, but the experience inspired Croser to establish his Argyle winery venture in Oregon in 1985.

One of the most important overseas ventures was David Hohnen's establishment of Cloudy Bay in Marlborough, at the top of New Zealand's south island. Hohnen's Cape Mentelle cabernets from Margaret River had burst onto the scene in the early 1980s by winning the Jimmy Watson trophy twice in a row, and he was inspired by influential young Victorian winemaker Stephen Hickinbotham to investigate the possibility of growing sauvignon blanc in New Zealand:

I had a lot of respect for Stephen. He was way out. I thought, gee, if he's on to it, there must be something good over there. Then in '83 there was an industry conference in Perth and I was simply too busy to attend, but three or four Kiwis arrived after the conference in a hired Falcon. They had some wine in the boot and we had a terrific session tasting my semillon and sauvignon from barrels. And then they brought these wines in. They were quite startling to me—the fruit characters. So in '84 I went to New Zealand and toured all of their regions and … picked Marlborough as the place we wanted to be.

In 1989, Penfolds dipped its toe in the water of the US wine industry by acquiring 50 per cent of a winery called Geyser Peak in California. 'Geyser Peak at that stage was actually known in the industry as Geyser Puke,' remembers Daryl Groom, the Australian winemaker sent over by Penfolds to help improve quality.

The wines … were sound but certainly not what everybody else was doing … There was a huge shift from generic wines to varietal wines. Chardonnay was the star. Big cabernets were starting to be made. It was a huge change in the wine industry. I think it was also a change, from what I gathered, from winemakers just being winemakers to winemakers becoming stars. Getting out in the industry—food and wine pairings, winemakers' dinners. There was a lot of press in the wine industry in those days.

This sense of excitement and possibility—and, yes, even glamour—that was rippling through the world wine industry in the 1980s attracted many young Australians. Keen to gain experience, graduates of the Roseworthy and Wagga winemaking schools were contracted by UK wine merchants and supermarkets and flown over to Europe to bring their up-to-date Aussie winemaking know-how to bear on technologically 'backward' wineries. This flock of flying wine-makers undoubtedly sparked a wine revolution in Europe well into the 1990s, but a legion of young Australians also returned clutching experiences and ideas they would then weave into their careers back home. Coonawarra winemaker Bruce Redman's account of his time in France in the 1980s is typical:

I went overseas for a couple of years. Did a vintage up in St-Estèphe in Bordeaux … I worked in a little place called Château Beau-Site, which was owned by some negociant wine dealers. It was really basic. Dirt floor. No stainless steel. Their fermentation was done in big wooden vats … very, very basic machinery. They didn't speak much English. In fact, I think the only [English] word that the guy who was the manager of the place could say was kangaroo. My French was limited but I knew a little bit. It was very interesting, though … The thing I enjoyed about it most was just the passion that people had for their wine. Even though they knew that it was not going to be a great year, they were very passionate about making their wine. Their life's work was making this wine. They didn't know any other lifestyle. That was really interesting. Also the other interesting thing, we found, that certainly didn't happen in Australia, was that they all used to have a glass of wine with morning tea and a glass of wine with lunch, and two or three glasses of wine with the meal in the evening. But it was never more than that. It was always a small glass and it wasn't as though it went on all day. It was strictly the glass of wine with the food.

James Halliday believes the 'flying winemaker' phenomenon has been hugely positive for the development of the industry: 'I'm yet to meet, or hear of, a flying winemaker who has come back to Australia [anything] other than enriched by the experiences that he or she gained overseas,' he says. 'They come back with a knowledge of the world, a knowledge of our competitors' strengths and weaknesses, a knowledge of the societies into which Australian wines will find their way, and I think we gain on the swings on that exchange far more than we lose on the roundabouts.'

Opposite: A vineyard in
St-Estéphe, Bordeaux, France

WINE AND WAR

'Hitler was a bit of a bastard'

World War I was a body blow to the Australian wine industry. Not only were many members of grape-growing and winemaking families among the 60 000 young Australians killed during the war, but the chaos in Europe decimated a booming export market: before the war, Australia had been well placed to provide wine to countries still reeling from the effects of the vine louse, phylloxera, which had wiped out many vineyards.

To make matters worse, many vineyards suffered terribly during the drought of 1916 to 1918, and wartime anti-German hysteria, particularly in South Australia, caused huge tension between the descendants of British and German settlers. According to Karl Seppelt, whose family had arrived in Australia from Silesia in 1849, 'A lot of the Germans in the Barossa Valley were in pretty serious trouble at that stage'; there were even mutterings of people having their wineries confiscated if they were not naturalised Australians.

In an effort to revive flagging spirits and provide a meaningful future for weary diggers, the government instigated a soldier settlement scheme, whereby returned servicemen were encouraged to take up a block of farming land rather than return to the city. Ex-soldiers were encouraged to plant vineyards in the relatively new irrigation districts along the Murray in South Australia and north-west Victoria, and along the Murrumbidgee in New South Wales. According to an article in *Wine and Spirit News* from 1919, government ministers roamed country regions looking for commercial grape-growing opportunities because the expansion of the wine industry was necessary out of 'duty to the Empire and to our noble Allies'.[1]

Reginald Langdon Buller, who had been a customs officer at Geelong prior to the war, returned from serving in the navy, looking for 'greener fields, or a different opportunity', says his grandson Andrew Buller. So he set out for Rutherglen:

To do so he had to get on a train and travel for two or three hours, and then get off, and then he had to take a horse ride to get [to] where the vineyard was. So he had to go to great pains to actually get here … I think at that particular time a lot of men returning from the First World War were being given parcels of land for returned servicemen. His happened to be one where a vineyard was involved. It wasn't given freely, he had to pay for it … He knew nothing about vineyards.

The post-war years also saw many European migrants leaving their poverty-stricken homelands and travelling to Australia, with some eventually establishing vineyards. And, as the clouds of a new war darkened the horizon during the late 1930s, a further wave of refugees, fleeing persecution and political unrest, arrived Down Under.

These refugees were not always welcomed with open arms. Oliver Shaul, for example, who arrived from Germany in 1939, would go on to become an influential hotelier and promoter of table wine, but initially found life hard in his adopted home. 'Australia,' says Oliver, 'was very isolated at that time

from the rest of the world,' and people like him were considered a threat and intrusion.

By 1939, the Australian wine industry had managed to reclaim much of the ground lost during World War I, but in September of that year with the declaration of another war, international trade ground to a halt. Ray Drew, then working for Hardys, says that, other than shipping wine to New Zealand, exports virtually ceased. (Ray also maintains that there was a shift in domestic sales and that some Hardys products were pushed aside and others favoured: 'The Manhattan Martini cocktail mixers virtually disappeared with the war and the sweet sherries took over'.) 'The Emu Wine Company,' adds Ben Chaffey, 'was [then] the biggest wine company in Australia, and in England but, of course, unfortunately the war undid it.'

Labour shortages became acute as men from rural communities across the country went off to fight. In McLaren Vale, d'Arry Osborn began work at his family's winery in 1943, and says it was a real struggle. 'I mean, it was war years and there was never enough labour. We were always behind.' At Bleasdale winery in Langhorne Creek, the Potts family were so short-staffed during the 1942 vintage that they were barely able to cope. Len Potts remembers his Uncle Arty coming into the winery on the evening before Good Friday:

'Come out and have a look at all the grapes you've got to put through,' [he said]. We looked down the lane and the loads went right back to where my mother used to live, which is about half a kilometre away.

There were horses and carts and all sorts of things lined up—wagons and trucks and utes, and they all had grapes in them and they all had to come through Bleasdale before we knocked off. I think we finished up about midnight that night.

Many wineries were forced to shift production from fortified wines to fuel. 'During the war, all went into abeyance,' says Richard Haselgrove. 'The distillation plant at Merbein was put over to producing power alcohol from molasses. Trainloads of tankers of molasses came down from Queensland to the Merbein railway station … That was [Dad's] wartime job, providing fuel to the Forces.'

Power alcohol was also produced at Seppeltsfield, along with vinegar, cordials and soft drinks. The Americans, who joined the war in 1941, had a thirst for citrus juice, so Seppelt converted a disused cannery in Nuriootpa and produced trainloads of canned juice for troops in the Pacific.

In other words, while the war had a disastrous impact on human life, local communities and international trade, it also provided some opportunities, and bred a generation of winemakers with unusual resilience and nous.

'The Australian wine industry was rudely interrupted by World War II,' says Richard Haselgrove, because the UK market was so important, and Australians at the time were not 'particularly wine drinkers'.

[But the industry] benefited from some of the problems of wartime because beer was restricted, spirits were no longer being imported, particularly Scotch,

and so wine became the alcoholic beverage of many who would otherwise have never been introduced to wine, I guess. So the war was a mixed blessing from the wine industry's point of view.

Forced to improvise in often-harsh conditions, some serving winemakers found inspiration in adversity. Ray Ward, who later worked for Woodley Wines and Yalumba, fought in the jungles of New Guinea, where he won his first gold medal—for 'jungle juice'. He was 'the only maker of jungle juice in our mob. So every time I made it I got a gold medal and a trophy. And it had a boot like a bloody mule. How we got out of it I'll never know. That was life.'

Other winemakers took full advantage of being posted away from their cellars. Ben Chaffey visited vineyards in Western Australia and talked with legendary winemaker Jack Mann, thanks to his posting with the RAAF. Another airman, Colin Gramp, found himself in England from 1943 to 1945, and would call on Orlando agents when he was given leave. 'These visits had a twofold advantage,' says Colin. 'Firstly, it was a wonderful opportunity to get to know the company's agents and to know what wines they were looking for, for marketing. And secondly, I had access to a goodly supply of wine and spirits for the squadron, and especially our crew.'

Colin—joined by John Seppelt and Drew Allen—then repatriated via California, where he visited wineries and gleaned all the latest trends during the 1945 vintage. 'It was a golden opportunity to look over a very modern-equipped wine industry,' he says, '[and]

gave me a great insight on how we could modernise the Australian wine industry through automation and bulk handling … Those three months in California were equivalent to one and a half years' oenological study.'

Many others returned with a similar sense of urgency and optimism. Ray Ward, for example, took advantage of the government's repatriation initiatives and completed the three-year Roseworthy course thanks to repat financial support.

'Hitler was a bit of a bastard,' says Ben Chaffey, 'but at least he sent us out to have a go on our own'.

CHAPTER 6

THE PIONEERS

New winemakers, new vineyards, new regions

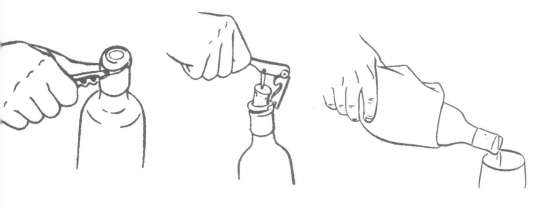

'Right. Off we go south.' I thought, 'Well, we must make some reasonable wine down there. Let's have a go.'

TOM CULLITY

Looking at a map of Australia's wine regions in the early years of the twentieth century is like looking at a map of the world in the Middle Ages. Just as whole tracts of the medieval world's surface are missing—yet to be discovered, charted and colonised—so, too, does an early map of the Australian wine landscape seem strangely empty to modern eyes.

On that early twentieth-century Australian wine map, you will see a few well-established warm-climate regions such as the Hunter Valley north of Sydney, the Swan Valley outside Perth, the Barossa and McLaren Vale near Adelaide, Rutherglen on the border of Victoria and New South Wales—all regions that can trace their history back to the 1850s or earlier. You will see the beginnings of a wine industry, too, along the inland rivers: the Riverland, Sunraysia, the Riverina, where new vineyards were beginning to supply grapes to the large wineries.

But you won't find regions that we now take for granted as producing some of this country's finest wines: Margaret River, the Mornington Peninsula, the Adelaide Hills, Tasmania, Orange, Beechworth. All these and more were only established in the last few decades of the century by a band of pioneers—doctors, farmers, dreamers, entrepreneurs—who fuelled what became known as the boutique boom, planting small vineyards, building small wineries and pursuing their passionate desire to produce their own wine. These people re-drew the Australian wine map; they discovered, charted and colonised country that, in many cases, had never before seen a vine.

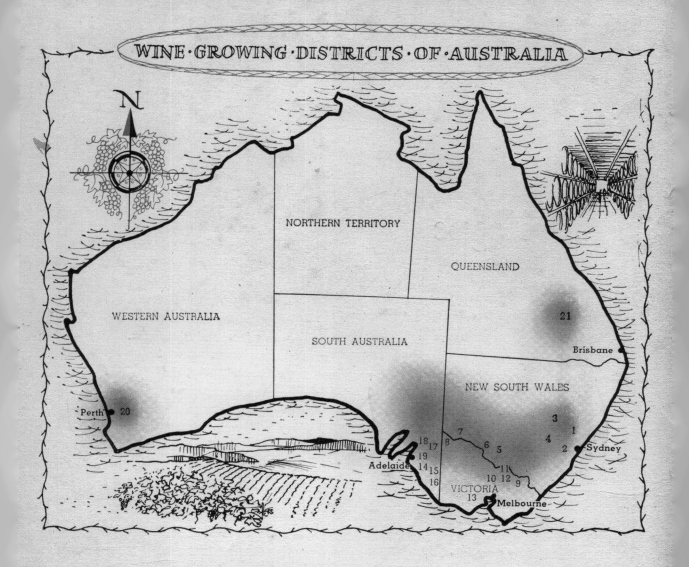

WINE·GROWING·DISTRICTS·OF·AUSTRALIA

NORTHERN TERRITORY

QUEENSLAND

WESTERN AUSTRALIA

SOUTH AUSTRALIA

NEW SOUTH WALES

Brisbane

Perth   20

Sydney

Adelaide

VICTORIA

Melbourne

LEGEND

1. Hunter Valley
2. Rooty Hill
3. Muswellbrook
4. Mudgee
5. Murrumbidgee Valley
6. Swan Hill
7. Robinvale
8. Murray Valley
9. Rutherglen, Wahgunyah Corowa
10. Tahbilk

11. Shepparton
12. Glenrowan-Milawa
13. Great Western
14. Southern Vales
15. Langhorne Creek
16. Coonawarra
17. Barossa Valley
18. Clare-Watervale
19. Adelaide Metropolitan
20. Swan Valley
21. Roma

The first sparks of the boutique boom occurred in the mid 1950s, when a few visionary lone wolves, such as Jean Miguet at Providence near Launceston, Claudio Alcorso at Moorilla Estate just outside Hobart, and Paul Osicka near Greytown in central Victoria, planted vineyards. But the first new boutique winemaker really to make an impression with the cognoscenti of Melbourne and Sydney was the larger-than-life surgeon and polymath Max Lake, who planted a vineyard—appropriately named Lake's Folly—in the Hunter Valley in 1963, inspiring a whole host of followers.

Before we get to Max, though, I want to give you an idea of how dramatic the boutique boom was by throwing some numbers at you. There are 2500-plus wine producers in Australia today. We take that for granted. But back in 1963, after more than a century and a half of the wine industry's existence, there were just 100 or so wineries. In the ten years following the planting of Lake's Folly, more than 150 winemakers opened new cellar doors. And by the mid 1980s, Australia could boast no fewer than 500 wineries, the vast majority of which were small, family-owned concerns in brand-new regions. That really is a remarkable revolution.

The Hunter stirs

The seeds of Max Lake's dream to own his own vineyard were planted in 1960, when the already-successful Sydney surgeon was visiting Melbourne wine merchant Doug Crittenden. Max, a passionate, gregarious and articulate wine lover, had started judging at wine shows under the tutelage of legendary winemakers such as Max Schubert and Colin Preece. So, Doug treated him to a bottle of Penfolds red from 1930.

The wine, from Penfolds' old Dalwood vineyard in the Hunter Valley, changed Max's life.

I had the wine at the age of thirty years—[it was] half cabernet, half petit verdot—and I thought that this is just incredible. I was starting to have a bit of knowledge about Bordeaux then and I thought that it's far better than any Bordeaux I'd tasted. And having worked out that it was grown 100 miles [60 kilometres] from Sydney, I thought, 'Whoopee! I'm not going to be doing surgery forever. Why don't I think about acquiring some [land] and growing stuff like this?' … I started looking for land immediately. It took three years.

A young Phil Ryan was working at the old McWilliam's family-owned Mount Pleasant winery in the Hunter in the late 1960s, and remembers this crazy and eager surgeon driving across the valley to get his wines analysed:

When his very first wines were made, he'd often come in the lab with samples. I've gone through various analyses for him. He'd sit on a stool and chat about what he was doing there [at Lake's Folly] and that sort of thing. I remember him as being quite visionary in terms of the Hunter. There were only six companies here then. So for Max to come in and do this was pretty exciting times.

When the first Lake's Folly wines appeared in the Sydney market in the late 1960s, they caused a sensation. Others quickly became keen to follow Max's lead and set themselves up as vignerons. The great wine promoter and entrepreneur Len Evans promptly established Rothbury Estate in the Hunter in 1968, and a couple of years later, one of Len's protégés, a Sydney lawyer called James Halliday, also took the plunge with a group of wine-loving mates and established Brokenwood.

James' recollections of the excitement and energy of those early pioneering years echo the experiences of many others among the new breed of boutique winemakers:

We got wind that there was to be an auction of four hectares of land in McDonalds Road, next to what is now Brokenwood … And we paid the then unheard-of price, which is much more than we intended to pay, of $1000 per acre … We had endless weekends up there at what we called 'stick picking'. It was like Jason's dragon teeth. The more sticks we picked, the more sticks there were remaining to be picked … And in 1971, we planted it and that was a horrendous experience for all of us … Shortly put, all jobs were physically very demanding. But we got it done. We planted 1 acre of shiraz and half an acre of cabernet. And then we followed up with more shiraz and the ridiculous bit of pinot. We made our first wine in 1973 … and we crushed 1 tonne of shiraz and half a tonne of cabernet.

Go west, young man: doctors and farmers dare to dream

Unlike Max Lake in the Hunter, who had initiated a renaissance in a very old region, the boutique pioneers in Western Australia planted vines in country that had never before made wine.

Vineyards had been a common sight in the hot suburbs of Perth since the early nineteenth century, but in the 1950s, experts started talking about the huge potential for vineyards in the cooler, viticulturally unexplored south-west of Western Australia, lending scientific weight to the hunches of legendary winemakers Jack Mann and Maurice O'Shea, both of whom said that, given their time again, they would plant vines in WA's remoter regions.

Californian viticulture professor Harold Olmo and local scientists John Gladstones and Bill Jamieson all identified Frankland River, Mount Barker

'Whoopee! I'm not going to be doing surgery forever. Why don't I think about acquiring some [land] and growing stuff like this?' … I started looking for land immediately. It took three years.
MAX LAKE

and Margaret River as being perfect for wine grapes. With advice coming from such eminent people, and faced with a slump in the agricultural sector, the WA Department of Agriculture decided to look into the proposals.

In 1965, Tony Pearse came across some strange visitors to Forest Hill, his remote Mount Barker farm. His wife, Betty Quick, remembers Tony coming home that evening and telling her that 'a funny thing had happened':

He said, 'Oh, couple of cars pulled up on the road and the chaps all piled out and ran over the paddocks.' So he thought that he'd better walk up and see what was going on, which he did. And there was Eddie Douglas—a chap that had worked in the apple industry—and he introduced Tony to some representatives of the Department of Ag, and they said that they were looking at soil sampling for this experimental vineyard. By that time, Tony was going off the farm six months of the year and I was left drenching sheep, treating flyblown sheep and with babies around my ankles. Like everybody else did. Money was tight … 'Well,' I said, 'grab it if it's offered to us'. Because it meant that it was something on our property … If it was a success, well, we had 5 acres of vines—two and a half of riesling, two and a half of cabernet—already up and going. If it was a failure, well, we had 5 acres of very well picked clean ground, and we had posts and strainers that we could use elsewhere on the farm … So that's how we became involved.

Bill Jamieson, you know, he was game. He took us on—we didn't know a thing. [I said] 'What sort of grapes are you planting?' 'Cabernet sauvignon, rhine riesling.' I said, 'What are they?' We'd never heard of this.

The year before the Department of Agriculture arrived in Mount Barker, a doctor called Tom Cullity had planted an experimental block of vines at his sister's and brother-in-law's farm at Burekup, over towards the south-west coast. Initially, Tom had been inspired by the old Houghton winemaker Jack Mann, who, says Tom, was like 'a prophet. He was like a Druid. And he was convinced about the capital importance of good wine, and nobody else in Western Australia gave a damn'.

Then, in 1965, Tom's brother gave him John Gladstones' thesis, which suggested Margaret River would be one of the best places in the world to grow cabernet sauvignon grapes. It changed Tom's life:

'Right. Off we go south.' I thought, 'Well, we must make some reasonable wine down there. Let's have a go.' Not realising what the problems were going to be. And so I got down there and [another doctor] Kevin Cullen was a great friend of mine. Had been for many years. And he very kindly used to put me up in his house and I went around digging holes in people's farms. I didn't know anything about anything. I'd read books on the subject. I'd asked a lot of questions.

To ask some of those questions, Tom drove across the Nullarbor to visit the imposing figures of John Fornachon and his assistant, Bryce Rankine, at the Wine Research Institute in Adelaide. 'Fornachon [looked] at me in a pretty impassive sort of way,' says Tom. 'And he said, "Well, come back in four years with some wine and we'll have a look at it and see what we think about it."'

With more enthusiastic encouragement from his doctor friends Kevin Cullen and Bill Pannell—both of whom would establish Margaret River vineyards of their own not long after—Tom found 20 acres (8 hectares) of pasture land selling for 'the astonishing sum of seventy-five bucks an acre … And they thought that they were robbing me. And I thought that they were, too'. This property would become the renowned wine estate Vasse Felix, but at the time planting a vineyard seemed like madness to the locals. Says Tom:

It was a poor area [economically]—dirt poor. There was hardly anybody there at Margaret River. It was a dead town. And they'd seen a whole lot of city slickers come down and they were going to do wonders … I suppose, behind my back, they'd have to make a bit of a joke … [about] some rich, mick doctor from Perth who's going to turn the world upside down. I know that I was thought to be starting a wife-swapping colony, and also a nudist colony … I remember leaning on the fence one evening and I was dead tired and a car went past and there was a sort of a Doppler effect. There was a woman leaning out of the car (one of the locals) and she said, 'Useleessss baaaastaaard.' It was a bit discouraging, because I *was* a useless bastard. I didn't know anything about fencing or anything. I had to learn.

Bill and Sandra Pannell had also been interested in planting a vineyard in the region ('Bill told me that he was very dirty and dark on me because he'd secretly been going to do it himself,' remembers Tom), and a couple of years later they found a site just to the north, with lovely gravelly soils and nice soft clays.

'I used to keep a shovel in the car,' says Bill, 'and any time I saw something that looked promising, I'd leap out and dig holes.' The Pannells managed to convince the patriarch of the family who owned the land to sell them a block—he said that 'if they wanted the area to progress they had to give people with ideas such as ours a go'—and in 1970, the first Moss Wood vines were planted, with help from Jack Mann. 'Jack … firmly believed that cabernet was the only grape allowed in heaven. And shiraz then was a bit out of favour. So we thought that, well, cabernet's the go. And Jack was very helpful. He had his vineyard workers collect the cuttings for us.'

This new wave of amateur vignerons, very few of whom had any viticultural training or winemaking experience, let alone farming nous, encountered plenty of problems. But, as John James, the founder of Margaret River vineyard Ribbon Vale, explains, there was strength in adversity:

[It] was a new country in terms of viticulture. There were problems. If it wasn't beetles eating [the vineyard], it was kangaroos eating it. If it wasn't that, if you did finally get grapes, it was birds eating it. Or the wind ripping it to shreds in the spring. And it really was a battle [but], like most battles, people are often united. So it was really good.

It wasn't all dilettante doctors diving into the wine game, though. Merv and Jude Lange were sheep farmers at Frankland, further inland from Margaret River, who were looking for a sideline for their farm during the slump in the wool industry of the late 1960s. 'At that time,' remembers Merv, 'there was just the first mention, or rumblings, of some sort of wine industry and it was suggested by a few that [Frankland] could be a good area for wine grapes. So we thought, "That'll do, we will plant some grapes …"'

After planting their Alkoomi vineyard, with advice from Bill Jamieson and Dorham Mann (winemaking son of Jack), the Langes quickly became fascinated

with wine—'hooked on what was in the bottle,' says Merv—and started getting involved in tastings with the very few producers that were in the southern part of the state at the time: vineyards like Vasse Felix, Moss Wood, Cullen and Forest Hill. They also inspired others, people like Bill Wignall, a vet in the remote coastal town of Albany, who planted pinot noir, despite the fact that many told him it would be hopeless.

'The challenge was there,' says Bill.

I remember Merv Lange saying, 'There's a lot of satisfaction in this business. I never had anybody say that that lamb I sold in the marketplace a few weeks ago was bloody beautiful or anything, but you'll get that with the wine.' And as soon as I released the first vintage I got calls from way out in the back country and New South Wales and all around the countryside. It was amazing.

Down south: cooler horizons

As Tom Cullity was planting cabernet sauvignon vines on his Margaret Valley Vasse Felix property—cuttings that had come, as on the Pannells' property, from the old Houghton vineyard in the Swan Valley—at a place called Legana in the Tamar Valley just outside Launceston, Graham Wiltshire was busy planting cabernet sauvignon vines from Coonawarra that had been supplied by Eric Brand of Laira.

The first wines from this experimental vineyard inspired Graham to establish the Heemskerk vineyard a few years later in the Pipers River region, to the east. And this in turn inspired David and Andrew Pirie, who had spent years doing research into the best place to make cool-climate wines, to plant a vineyard next door. As in Western Australia, says Graham, early challenges inspired collaboration:

We bought the property [in 1974] and started developing it. David Pirie, with Andrew, had bought the adjoining property, which in the previous ten or fifteen years had been cleared, but it was all covered with rows of fallen timber, having been heavily forested country. Ferns, regrowth and wallabies. So [Andrew] came to me and said, 'Look, we haven't got any suitable land, or any water, to grow our propagation material' … So we put a nursery in at the old Legana vineyard … and then grew the propagation material, which was a mixture of cabernet, riesling and the old McWilliam's clone of chardonnay. There was no pinot at that stage.

It's an important point. In the 1970s and early 1980s, cabernet was king. The established classic cabernets from Coonawarra, and the new wave of cabernets emerging from Western Australia and the renascent Victorian wine regions such as the Yarra Valley and Bendigo, were thrilling wine lovers across the country. Chardonnay was still a new, alternative grape, and very few people were interested in pinot noir—or even thinking about the potential for blending the two to produce high-quality sparkling wine, à la champagne. So it was hard for pioneers such as Graham Wiltshire to find the best ways to grow their grapes and make wine.

It was real pioneering stuff. Even though I would make frequent trips to the mainland and talk to people, the expertise had very little to do with cool-climate viticulture. Or cool-climate winemaking, if it came to that. It was something completely different. [Dr Tony] Jordan had a better appreciation than most people because he had the opportunity to see a lot of action in New Zealand at that stage and good contacts with [viticulturist] Richard Smart. And so he helped, especially on the winemaking side. But viticulture was almost an unknown thing in Australia for cool climate … We were having trouble with acceptable yields and quality, with chardonnay and pinot and especially with cabernet. We kept getting these green, herbaceous characters almost to a cabbagey stage in a cool year, which were just undesirable … And from that I thought that, well, we're going to get the occasional bad year in this area, we need to use that material for a different end use in those cooler years. And sparkling wine seemed to be the way to go. There was not much sparkling wine grown in Australia in the mid '80s, so it did look as though it could've been a proposition.

Through his wholesale distributor, Graham made contact with the champagne house of Roederer, who were interested in expanding into the New World, and had already invested in California. Graham sent samples of some sparkling base wines he'd been playing with, and that piqued their interest enough to come out and have a look. This would eventually lead to the formation of a joint venture between Heemskerk and Roederer and the development of the Jansz sparkling wine brand in the late 1980s.

Meanwhile, just across Bass Strait, Victoria was experiencing its own boutique wine revolution. As well as the revival of old nineteenth-century regions such as Bendigo (kickstarted by the establishment in 1969 of Balgownie Estate by pharmacist and polymath Stuart Anderson—Victoria's answer to Max Lake) and the Yarra Valley (like Margaret River, the first Yarra vineyards in the 1960s were planted by doctors such as John Middleton at Mount Mary and Peter McMahon at Seville Estate), new, cool regions such as the Mornington Peninsula began to emerge in the 1970s.

In the mid 1980s, Victoria's cool-climate boutique winery boom received a high-profile boost when champagne house Moët et Chandon and the country's leading wine critic, James Halliday, both decided to establish a presence in the Yarra Valley.

In 1985, James was leading a particularly hectic life, often working two vintages a year—one at his Brokenwood vineyard in the Hunter, one in Burgundy—as well as working as a partner at law firm Clayton Utz. Initially, he intended to simply buy some grapes each year from the Yarra's growing number of vineyards, and make wine in friends' wineries. But then the spectacular hillside property where the Coldstream Hills winery and the Hallidays' house now sit came on the market.

I'd said to Bailey Carrodus [at Yarra Yering, just below Coldstream Hills] that if something came up in this particular part of the Yarra Valley I'd be very interested in at least knowing what it was going for. And I'd said the same to the Churches at Warramate [next door]. It was Jack Church who rang me up at the office and said that there's an auction sign just gone up on the property. So Tony Jordan and I had been down at Mornington Peninsula mucking around with the wine on that day. We drove up here in the middle of the winter of 1985 and waited at the house down the front [near the road]. It was pissing down rain. Terrible weather. And the agent didn't turn up. We were about to leave—I'd rung the agent up and found the expected value … and this had got me interested because I couldn't

Above: Mount Mary vineyard in the Yarra Valley, established by pioneer John Middleton in the 1960s

believe how cheap it was. But no-one was there … Tony said, 'Well, why don't we just check that it's not the one up the hill.' I said, 'It can't possibly be. Not at that sort of price.' Anyway, we took the fifty-yard drive to see, indeed, that the auction sign was for this [other] place. We came up there and the agent was just about to go. He'd given us for dead. And it was actually a weekend, a Sunday. And on the spot I said, 'I'm going to buy it.' And contracts were exchanged on the Tuesday. I rang up the bank manager and said, 'Look, I'm signing a $25 000 deposit. Don't bounce it whatever you do. I know I don't have an overdraft but I'll sort something out.' And those were the glory days of merchant banking when everything was possible.

Like so many of the new boutique vignerons in the 1980s and since, James was swept up in the dream, and borrowed heavily to finance a winery. Then the neighbouring property came up for sale in late 1987 and, to fund that purchase, James decided on a small public float.

But October 1987, you might remember, was when the sky really fell in with that massive decline in stock … and start of the big depression. But initially, it was only the stock market. I kept on saying to my merchant bank friend, 'Look, is this thing going ahead or not?' He said, 'Look, don't worry … It's nothing. Forget it. Stop bothering me. We'll do it.' And indeed the prospectus was issued in December, and it was the first company to list after the stock market crash in Australia.

Into the hills: new regions emerge in South Australia

Well-established wineries in the Barossa had started the move to find cooler climates for riesling in the early 1960s. The Germanic styles of sweetish white wine popular in the 1950s and early 1960s—wines labelled 'Moselle' and 'Hock'—relied on technology such as temperature control to coax delicate flavours from sometimes coarse-tasting grapes from the warmer climate Barossa Valley. Orlando's Colin Gramp reasoned that if the grapes were grown in conditions similar to those found along the Mosel and Rhine rivers in Germany, which were often quite stony, cold vineyard sites, then you could produce a wine with *natural* delicacy and finesse. So he found a particularly tough site in the cooler hills above the Barossa, planted a vineyard and called it Steingarten:

[There was] hardly any soil on the surface but we broke it up. It was the schist rock formation, which was ripped up by a Caterpillar hoe. And then, unfortunately, the larger pieces had to be broken by the stone hammer. I wouldn't like to mention what our workmen thought of me at the time ... [But] these vines, because of these harsh conditions and growing among rock, produced a [wine] that was delicate, flinty. The flavour was there but it was delicate and it was well balanced with the natural acid.

At about the same time, Yalumba planted riesling at the historic Pewsey Vale site high up in the Eden Valley—a site that had first been planted in 1847, but was pulled out in the 1920s. Norman Hanckel, Yalumba's production manager at the time, first raised the idea of replanting Pewsey Vale with the property's owner, Geoffrey Angas Parsons, at a function:

We [were drinking] these beautiful [South Australian] rieslings, [but] he insisted that I buy him German white wines at the dinner party. So all the way through he drank two bottles of expensive German wine at our expense. Towards the end of the party I said to him, 'You could get wine of this quality made in Australia if you'd let me have some of your vineyard.' And that's how it started off. He said, 'Well, come around tomorrow morning and I'll give you, personally, 40 acres.' And so I fronted up the next morning after the party. And then I suggested to him instead that it would be a lot easier to make it up to 200 acres and go into partnership with Yalumba, which he did.

By the late 1970s, innovative winemakers were beginning to look beyond the traditional stalwart South Australian varieties of riesling and shiraz to the up-and-coming cool-climate varieties such as chardonnay, sauvignon blanc, merlot and pinot noir. As a result, winemakers started looking seriously at the Adelaide Hills.

The hills had been home to a few small vineyards in the nineteenth century, but for most of the twentieth they had been a centre for stone fruit and apple production. Fresh from their experience in Germany and now running their family winery in the Eden Valley, Prue and Stephen Henschke were keen to explore viticulture in the area. 'Peter Dry and Dick Smart at Roseworthy were just getting into new definitions for site selection,' says Prue. 'Going out beyond the old regions. And had written a booklet on site selection. So I took that information and we looked around because I had this feeling that if the vines were less stressed during summer, the flavour profiles would be more intense.'

The Henschkes looked at many areas, but settled on the Adelaide Hills because it was close to their winery at Keyneton.

I can remember having discussions with Dick Smart about moving the winery. I said, 'You can't move a century-old stone structure.' He said, 'Well, what value is it?' I said, 'There's every value in this beautiful old building. It's been here for a century and it's our life' … We saw [the Lenswood] property up for sale. And it was covered in apples at that stage. Apples, cherries and pears. So we rang up and made enquiries. It looked a bit steep but we said, 'Well, [if] the Germans can cope with steep hills, then we can.' So we eventually bought it … with a working apple orchard on it. I ran the orchard for two seasons. It was incredibly hard work … Then the bushfire of 1983 [Ash Wednesday] came through and actually burnt the whole orchard flat to the ground. The wind change occurred at our boundary. So it got a double dose to make sure that everything was removed. We had two small plots of vines on it and they were planted in black plastic and because they were green they didn't burn. So the only thing that was left were the vines on the whole property … We used every ounce of German technology—or German methodology—we could use. We used green subcultures [cover crops] in the mid rows. We went to vertical shoot positioning [for more sun exposure in the vine canopy]. We used our German clones for riesling and we were very concerned about what to plant there. Clonal selection was really important. Yes, the whole thing was done very much for what the landscape required because it's over 1100 millimetres [of] rainfall.

Prue points out that a handful of others planted new vineyards in the hills at the time: people such as Brian Croser, Tim Knappstein and Geoff Weaver, all well-known, respected winemakers with established reputations. So the region 'started up with guts and determination. It was a group of people, possibly from the same vintage, I suppose, getting into research and development for a new area. Really pioneering something new. And it was exciting and fulfilling'.

ALL IN THIS TOGETHER
Cooperation, collaboration and community

One of the most important factors behind the story of Australian wine is the extraordinary spirit of open collaboration that exists throughout the industry, whether it's individual grape growers or winemakers happily sharing the tricks of their trade with other growers or makers, or groups of vignerons working together to promote their wines in export markets.

In Australia's older, traditional wine regions, the collaborative spirit was often forged out of adversity. The Hunter Valley is perhaps one of the most dramatic examples of this: established in the nineteenth century primarily because of its proximity to Sydney and Newcastle, it is not really ideal grape-growing country—as generations of vignerons will ruefully attest. Mount Pleasant winemaker Phil Ryan is blunt about how the environmental challenges of the region have inspired a sense of community:

The Hunter's an extremely difficult place to make wine consistently, and grow grapes. As we all know, it rains at all the wrong times of the year and then it doesn't rain [much for the rest] of the year. So the people here really do feel challenged all the time. There's never an easy part of the year, so that brings people close together. That's really what knits the group together here, just knowing how difficult it is.

In more remote regions, such as Coonawarra, the tyranny of distance also promoted close ties and warm hospitality. This was certainly true in the nineteenth and early twentieth centuries, but Coonawarra's sense of isolation continued well into the 1960s and

beyond (some say it's still a defining feature of the place). David Moss, who worked with the Department of Agriculture in Coonawarra during the 1970s, remembers the excitement that rippled through the local winemaking community whenever other wine folk visited:

In those days I used to have groups of people turn up down here, coming to have a look at Coonawarra ... When that happened I'd just ring Colin [Kidd from Lindemans], as Chairman of the Viticultural Council, and we'd go. Either Colin or Vic [Patrick from Mildara] would hop on [the bus]. They all knew as much about everyone else's vineyard as their own. There was no worry; the bus would just drive through anyone's vineyard. Might be Colin on and they'd go through Wynns and all the rest of it ... It was just open to everyone. It was a terrific feeling.

Ray Beckwith of Penfolds remembers a similar collegiate feeling among winemakers in the Barossa during the 1950s. Ray recalls regular meetings of the Bacchus Club, a dining and drinking society made up mainly of people in the wine industry in the region.

You'd talk among yourselves on what's going on with methods of production; with agreements and disagreements, of course. Winemakers have all got their own ideas and if you say that you think that you ought to do it this way, the other winemaker might say, 'Well, I don't agree with you.' But, okay, that's the way it is.

There is a very strong tradition of sharing information through mentoring in the Australian wine industry; both official, through company-organised education programs, and unofficial. Many winemakers, for example, talk with affection of Jack Kilgour, who had a long career at Stonyfell, Tatachilla and Hardys from the 1940s onwards, and sounds more like a character from a novel than from real life.

'He was a grumpy old man,' remembers Brian Croser. 'He was a grumpy old Scotsman who had been jilted in life by circumstance, but he had an enquiring scientific mind and he wouldn't accept second-rate answers.'

'It was very interesting to work with him,' says Grant Burge, who encountered Jack in his twilight years. 'You could have a half-an-hour conversation with him and it would probably save you three years of actual work … He'd say, "Oh, look, I tried that thirty years ago and this was the result." And in half an hour you'd learn everything … [from] the last thirty years.'

Greg Trott tells a lovely story about Jack:

I remember one day we'd just walked out of a board meeting, out of the cellar door area, and we were standing around there and Blacker [the winery engineer] came up and said, 'Hullo, Trotty' … I said, 'What are you doing?' He said, 'I've got to fix this bloody pump up. It's got this peculiar washer. I bet it's gone again.' Anyway … he came back about five or six minutes later … He said, 'Well, I'm going off to get a washer.' Jack said, 'What sort of washer do you need?' He went into his coat pocket and brought out this ring of washers, and he said, 'I think this is the one that'll fit.' And it was. Unbelievable!

Left (above): The Blass family—Peter, Patricia, Fritz, Hanni and Wolf

Left (below): A joint venture wine export to Holland, left to right—Peter Wall, Wolf Blass, Dennis Reimann, John Braniff, James Wark and Mark Hall Smith

Opposite: Current and past members of the Coonawarra Vignerons Association, originally formed in 1979

John Bird captures the importance of such mentoring and passing-on as he ponders the importance of working at Penfolds with giants such as Ray Beckwith and Max Schubert in the 1970s:

I owe a lot to those fellows. You've still got to have a feel for it yourself. That inner something, if you like. But it was very, very interesting in more ways than one, working closely by them … you were gradually brought up with the fact that these are the types of laboratory analyses we want to see in our wines. And they taught you about why. All those kinds of things. And the style of wine. Maturation methods and how

to achieve this. But again, you've still got to have a bit of a feel for it yourself, too. Let's face it, we've all got our own ideas, and you might just add something to what you've been taught, or erase something that you think might be superfluous.

By the late 1970s, whole winemaking communities began to make more of a concerted effort to group together and help each other. Bruce Redman of Redman Wines in Coonawarra explains that while the region's winemakers had 'gone out and been competitors in the marketplace, when it comes to a viticultural and winemaking production level, we've had to rely on our next-door neighbours for advice, because to go somewhere else is very difficult.'

[That's why] the Coonawarra Vignerons Association was formed in 1979. It was formed with about six or eight members originally. Basically, it was formed by people who had cellar door sales in Coonawarra and with a charter of attracting more visitors to the area. … [The] advantage—or disadvantage—we've got is that we're all next door to each other, whether we like it or not. There's no distance between us, so everyone knows what the other person's doing … So we've built up a great rapport and a great strength of community in the region.

The old-timers in the small, close-knit communities in traditional wine regions such as the Clare Valley also welcomed the influx of new boutique winemakers in the 1970s and 1980s with open arms. Brother

John May of the venerable Sevenhill winery says the region's winemakers were always sharing ideas and helping each other during that period:

I remember a grower that was battling to get his fruit in and I went down with our front-end loader and spent all Sunday driving the front-end loader … throwing the grapes in … We did a lot of that … [When Andrew and Jane Mitchell won their first gold medal at the Brisbane Wine Show] quite a number of us raced down to the Mitchells with bottles in hand and had a celebratory drink. That's the sort of thing that people did.

By the time the export boom took off in the late 1980s and early 1990s, Australian winemakers had not only established a very strong system of collaborative networks, but they also made sure this united front was on display to the rest of the world. As Viv Thomson of Best's Great Western puts it:

I'm sure this is the reason why as an export industry we've been so successful. We've worked together on the wine side of things, we've worked together on the viticultural side of things and also we work together on the marketing side of things. We might go our own ways but I wouldn't like to repeat how many times I've worked on stands overseas and promoted—because the fellow wasn't there or something [like that]—and sold wines from the Barossa Valley, or the Hunter or somewhere like that, because he was the next stand to mine. We work together on that sort of thing. I know it just doesn't seem to happen in other industries.

CHAPTER 7

SHOW AND TELL

Introducing Australians to Australian wine

Oh, hullo. Good afternoon. Do come in. We have our wines set out on the table. You can help yourself to them but make sure that you can walk out by the time you go.
MICKIE CLIFFORD

You can have the most advanced grape-growing techniques, the most innovative winemaking technology and the most up-to-date research in the world. You can be producing the finest wines in the history of humanity. But the whole shebang comes grinding to a halt if nobody knows about your wines or, worse, doesn't want to buy them.

The success of Australian wine in Australia—the huge changes in a whole society's drinking habits and tastes—could not have happened without the inventiveness, hard work and dedication of some exceptionally talented, even visionary, retailers, promoters, writers and marketers.

What I find fascinating is the very close relationships and blurred boundaries that have always existed between these sectors of the wine trade in Australia, especially in the 1960s and 1970s, at the height of the wine boom: writers also worked as promoters; retailers were also writers; promoters also made wine. As in other areas of the Australian industry, these cosy relationships undoubtedly engendered a collegiate spirit of cooperation that helped the wine industry grow rapidly. But these intimate connections also led to a culture of boosterism—of uncritically supporting the industry, of talking up the potential rather than cautiously pointing out the pitfalls—that has been very hard to shake, even in the recent highly challenging years of the industry's history.

Wine in the bottle shop: from old-fashioned merchants to discount liquor barns

Doug Crittenden's story is typical of how wine retailing changed during the 1950s and 1960s from licensed grocers mostly selling large quantities of sherry, port and sweet white, to 'proper' wine merchants selling an eager, thirsty public bottles of riesling, claret and burgundy.

Doug grew up in his father Oscar's well-known licensed grocer's store in Melbourne, and spent the years of World War II washing bottles and serving customers. After a trip to Europe, where he studied and visited widely in Germany, Bordeaux and London, Doug returned to Australia with a new vision for the store. Faced with a wine trade dominated by cartels and price-fixing—one big brewery threatened to cut supply if he didn't agree to their terms—Doug decided to bottle more wines under the Crittenden brand.

Initially, the market was primarily for fortified wines, as it had been in his father's day: 'There wouldn't be a week go by that there wouldn't be a truck come down from the Riverland with six hogsheads of sherry on. This is when we were at the height of our business. And some weeks [it was] more than that.'

After a while, it occurred to Doug that there might be more money to be made in table, rather than fortified, wine. After all, he reasoned, when people buy

Above: Australian Wine Week promotion, Sydney, 1948

fortified wine they only buy a bottle. But when they buy table wine they buy a half-dozen or dozen bottles at a time. And yet, both had the same margin. Doug also knew that if he were going to convince people to change their buying habits from sweet sherry to light table wines, he was going to have to offer them something special. So he began sourcing wines direct from the winemakers' cellars.

On a Monday morning I used to catch the seven o'clock from Melbourne—or seven-thirty, I think it was then—and I'd pick up a hire car at Adelaide airport. And I'd go down to McLaren Vale first … We were always regularly buying in those days from Cud Kay [at Amery], his bulk shiraz. And we used to call that McLaren Vale Shiraz. We used to get about six hogsheads over at a time. I'd call to see Cud and taste from some of his casks, to see if he had anything special that he would let me have that was a little better in quality. Might be a small run, just a couple of hogsheads that we could run off as a special, or something like that … Then on the Tuesday I'd always do Adelaide and surrounding districts … to Hardys at Mile End … They were the first to make me up a blend for a rosé, and I looked at several samples … I'd call on Peter Lehmann and, of course, you'd get caught up there and he was at Saltram at the time. He was one of my big suppliers … I got very pally with Brother John Hanlon [at Sevenhill] and he used to come over for the football and I'd entertain him. And, of course, I'm not a very religious person, I'm not even a Catholic, but it used to amaze everybody that

I was agent for Sevenhill [because they were better known at the time for altar wine]. And, of course, I was agent for Cyril Henschke and I used to go down and buy bulk from Cyril, too. And we used to label it under Henschke.

With that kind of commitment and legwork, and with the quality of wines that these legendary vignerons were able to supply him, Doug soon converted a whole generation of Melbourne wine drinkers to the delights of table wine. And he wasn't alone: a small but dedicated group of retailers, restaurateurs and hoteliers were active in the 1950s and early 1960s, busily converting as many customers as they could—people such as Jimmy Watson, of the eponymous wine bar in Melbourne, whose buying trips took him to Rutherglen and Clare; merchants such as Johnny Walker and Doug Lamb, both in Sydney, who supported winegrowers in the Hunter Valley; and restaurateurs such as Hermann Schneider and Oliver Shaul.

In 1960, a brash young man called Len Evans started working for Frank Christie at Sydney's Chevron Hilton Hotel. Len's infectious enthusiasm for wine and unwavering self-confidence saw him promoted to assistant general manager within two years. It was the start of a career in hospitality, marketing, winemaking and show judging that would change the face of Australian wine forever. Says Len:

That was my university … And we had the best cellar in Australia. There's no question of that. Best cellar, I think, that's probably ever been bred in Australia.

We had huge table wine sales because we had a huge restaurant. We had the 650-seat Silver Spade, an 800-seat ballroom, an 800-seat lounge, and consequently they had a lot of wine. I became the darling of the industry, as I sold lots and lots of their wine. People like Lindemans, Penfolds, Seppelt, Orlando, Thomas Hardy (very important to me), all very much sought my company—and Yalumba—because they had wine to sell me, and because they could see that I was going in a direction in which they weren't very strong [table wine].

This new breed of merchants and spruikers was enormously successful at spreading the message, and by the early 1970s, the table wine boom was in full swing, helped along by innovations in packaging such as the flagon and the cask. The retail market then took another dramatic turn when the Whitlam government introduced its Trade Practices Act, putting a stop to wholesale price fixing. This led to a wave of discounting across the retail sector, as new bottle shops opened across the country and tried desperately to compete with each other.

According to Hardys' Ray Drew, the effect of discounting was much more profound, leading eventually to the extreme consolidation and virtual duopoly of today's wine retail market. Ray remembers dealing with one large discounting company in particular: 'They screwed so hard that there wasn't much in it. So as we were in business to make a profit, we pulled out of that and let them go their own way.'

The quantity discounts became quite a marketing tool. 'Buy it by the semi-trailer and you got X discount' and so on. And this, of course, caused group hoteliers and retailers to merge—get together. Form their buying groups to get the quantity discounts. Buying power became quite a new adjunct to the industry.

Promotion, publicity and the press

Australia has long had a tradition of 'gentlemen wine writers': nineteenth-century doctors and vineyard owners, such as Alexander Kelly in McLaren Vale and Hubert de Castella in the Yarra Valley, who wrote treatises and histories in their 'spare time'.

In the middle years of the twentieth century, one such gentleman wine writer, Walter James, emerged to pen a number of books that spoke, in elegant prose, to the few cognoscenti then interested in fine wines and the pleasure of the table. 'I knew him personally and he was a bit of an eccentric man,' remembers restaurateur Hermann Schneider:

His writing was very much in the English style, but it was witty, it was charming, it had depths of knowledge and it wasn't commercial. I really must say that I'm

sure he gave a lot of the people enjoyment. I get disappointed sometimes when I look up [modern] wine critics and even wine books and it is too analytical and too technical. Walter James had an understanding.

Historian and writer Valmai Hankel believes that Walter James was 'one of the greatest wine writers Australia has ever had'. But in the 1950s, he was a lone voice: there were no newspaper wine columns, no consumer-focused wine magazines. And this made it hard for winemakers, keen to promote table wines, to get their message out to the people. Yes, a couple of local wine festivals such as the biennial vintage celebration in the Barossa had sprung up, and the industry organised an annual Wine Week promotion in the major capital cities. But wine wasn't a constant topic of conversation as it is now.

So, in 1955, the Australian Wine Board employed a full-time promotions officer whose name was Harry Palmer. Harry's first task was to initiate an advertising campaign, urging people to 'take wine out of the cupboard and to put it on the table'.

'There was no table wine market,' Harry remembers. 'The intention of the national advertising campaign was to promote the sale mainly of table wine. It seemed to work because every campaign they ran, it showed some result in the sales figures. It pleased the industry; it was the kick-off.'

As well as advertising campaigns, some in the wine industry realised the importance of taking the bottles to the people. Bernie Stephens and Don Rogers of the Wine and Brandy Producers Association in South Australia started promoting wine in suburban shopping centres. 'Don and I were the first ones, I think, in Australia to take wine into … the malls,' says Bernie.

We'd usually set up a table like the old British square. You know, facing in all directions. We'd set the wines up and people would come and have a look. Mostly it was purely curiosity that attracted them in the first instance, but it got them interested in wine. I think it was a great promotion effort. It got people talking about wine. In the early years it was curiosity that brought them to the tables and then they all wanted to have a taste. You'd usually get some funny comments. I always remember being at the Marion shopping centre when it first opened and having the tables all set up there. I was helping behind the tables with the hostesses, and this lady came down, and I said, 'What would you like to try?' She said, 'Anything to get the taste of that vermin out of my mouth.' She'd just had a vermouth. And we had some funny experiences. We always took glass tasting glasses, basically sherry glasses. They had to be washed all the time. That was part of the job for the hostesses to rush off with a bucket of glasses and wash them all and dry them and bring them back. This was a continuous operation when you're dealing with hundreds of people. And we always lost glasses. I remember seeing a young woman with a pusher and a baby one day and saw her finish her taste, and then she lifted the flap of the carry-bag and put the glass in and went to walk off. I just said to her, 'Excuse me, madam, but I think you have one of our glasses in your bag.' She said, 'No, I haven't.' I said, 'Would you rather I get the security man to come and have a look? But I think you have got one.' Anyway, she finally gave in. She opened her bag and gave me back six. She'd got the half-dozen she wanted and was just about to take off with them. She was quite sober. She just wanted the glasses. Really, it was an experience.

During that period our whole theme in promotion was not just to get out there and flog a product and get everybody just buying it and drinking it; our total attitude in our promotional activity at that time was wine in moderation and in association with food … And the other phrase that I used so often was when people would talk about which wines, you know, do you like, what should we do? I used to say, 'The best wine on the table is the one you like.' And so that was our total attitude in promotion.

Meanwhile, Len Evans, not content with introducing people to wine at the Chevron Hotel, also started to write about it, with his first column appearing under the name of Cellarmaster in the *Bulletin* in 1962, and other columns in other papers following not long after.

The Australian Wine Board took great interest in Len's writing and its influence. Len remembers recommending in the *Bulletin* one of d'Arry Osborn's red wines that he particularly liked, and d'Arry sold out of it in a week. What's more, he sold out of *all* his red. 'I mean, [that was the] extraordinary power of the columns in those days. There weren't many columns. There were hardly any columns, so consequently that column had a great push.'

Realising that the charismatic Evans could be an enormous boon to spreading wine's message, the board lured him away from the Chevron and hired him as promotions officer. Len's first contribution was to set up wine information bureaus in each state—bureaus that quickly learned how to use the media to get people interested in wine. As well as continuing to write his own columns, Len hired writers to contribute wine articles.

I had to convince the editors that they should have a wine column. I then had to convince the radio stations that they should have a radio program. Most of it came off, but it was all hard work. I can remember the *Australian* [starting up] and I flew to Canberra to talk to Walter Kroner, who was the editor of the *Australian*. 'Why would we want a wine column?' I said, 'Well, you can be the leader then, can't you?'

Frank Margan, one of the first men Len hired for the Sydney bureau, recalls the excitement and energy that Evans brought to the job of wine promotion:

I must've written something because Len Evans rang me up and said, 'I like that story you wrote. Can we have lunch?' 'Yes, sure.' You know, lunch was my favourite hobby … Len [had] formed the Australian Wine Bureau, with him running it, and I was [to be] his writer. So we then took off in this clapped-out old Holden … to 'do' the Australian wine industry. We did eighty-six wineries in two weeks. We had just a fabulous time.

Len's team of writers—including Frank Doherty in Melbourne and Jack Ludbrook in Adelaide, as well as Frank Margan in Sydney—started churning out articles, increasing the awareness of wine. 'I wrote a lot of wine columns,' says Frank. 'I was a very fast writer. I just picked every little paper in Australia that wanted space filled … Wine was starting to become a kind of fashion thing.'

> I had to convince the editors that they should have a wine column. I then had to convince the radio stations that they should have a radio program.
> **LEN EVANS**

Orlando's Perry Gunner says that Len Evans was everywhere in the 1960s. 'He was prevalent on television and in the press and never lost an opportunity to promote wine, but in that real outgoing style, and I think that the wine industry hadn't been used to those sorts of characters back then that were so very outgoing. I think the community lapped it up.'

They certainly did. Len likes to point out that when he started working for the board, Australians drank one bottle of table wine per head per year—and when he left, just a few years later, they were drinking six.

'[Len] was the ideal man for the job we wanted, which was to get to the retail trade, to the consumer, and that's what happened,' says Harry Palmer. 'The press themselves started to take more interest in wine. This sort of mushroomed … Gradually the consumption was reversed and table wines took over from ports and sherries … That was how the Australian scene started.'

Evans and his team weren't the only ones writing about wine in the 1960s. Melbourne wine merchant Dan Murphy had a column in the *Age* (concerns about conflict of interest were clearly less of an issue than they might be today), and in 1960, a Melbourne doctor, Sam Benwell, published a wonderful book called *Journey to Wine in Victoria*. Benwell's beautifully evocative pilgrimage around the state's wine regions, very much in the stylistic tradition of the gentlemen wine writers of the past, was a surprising success. So, the publisher approached another doctor—and fledgling vigneron—Max Lake, to write a similar book about the Hunter Valley. This, too, reached a wide audience, thirsty for knowledge, and inspired Max to write another.

I'd started to become really serious and I had sent out questionnaires all around Australia for what I presumed, in my ego and ignorance, to be the classic wines. I defined what I thought classic was and that's actually held up pretty well. It had to be made for ten years at least. It had to be a consistent style, not all over the place. And it had to be three excellent years in ten. The questionnaires came back from forty different wineries. Some weren't answered. Some were answered very fully. And I wrote *Classic Wines of Australia* for Jacaranda and it was published in 1966. It kept getting reissued and reissued and reissued … I was invited to join the boards of wine companies. I'd go to the board meetings and there would be the *Classic Wines of Australia* books around the place. Women rang me to say they slept with this by their bedside tables. Unbelievable! It was the right book at the right time. And I was dogmatic, authoritarian, opinionated, and there was no-one to argue with me.

At the coalface: wine and food clubs, cellar doors, festivals and tourism

The 1950s and 1960s saw a grassroots revolution take place across Australia as people, newly enamoured of this thing called wine, gathered in groups for a spot of like-minded appreciation—over lunch or dinner, of course.

Sydney wine merchant and restaurateur Johnnie Walker was one of the founding members in the 1950s of a Food and Wine Society, which went on regular trips to the Hunter Valley to visit the few winemakers then toiling away—people such as the Tullochs, and legendary vigneron Maurice O'Shea, in his tin shed with its dirt floor.

In Adelaide at around the same time, it had become a tradition for members of the wine industry to gather at the Imperial Hotel every Friday lunchtime. 'Other diners would see this industry table drinking their wines, discussing wines, and [they] became interested,' says Ray Drew. As a result, Ray and seven of his mates decided to form a Beefsteak and Burgundy Club, for trade and public alike, which met at the hotel.

Des Leahy, the then owner/proprietor … would buy the prize-winning carcasses in beef competitions and hang them for several weeks and then serve them at these … Club dinners. I think that's part of the reason the name, Beefsteak, became synonymous with the Beefsteak and Burgundy Clubs. Food played a tremendous part. We not only discussed wines, we discussed food, because, in my opinion, wine can only complement food.

Bernie Stephens tells a similar story of the Epicurean Club, which had begun to meet at Loxton in South Australia's Riverland. As well as managers from local wineries, says Bernie, the group included 'a lot of the local dentists and the doctors'.

They were the sorts of townspeople that became interested and joined, probably in the initial stages for the social side of things, like you do in a country town … They were good fun nights. And it was interesting to have masked wines. You developed a palate appreciation of wines in those sorts of clubs. They were great. And they were good wine promotion. Everybody that went through an Epicurean Club or a Beefsteak and Burgundy Club never ever had an empty cellar.

In many ways, without this new interest in wine fostered by these enthusiastic groups, all the writing about wine by Len Evans and others might have fallen on deaf ears. The two developments were running in tandem, feeding off each other. Ray Drew believes that the growing interest in wine was 'mainly word of

> Everybody that went through an Epicurean Club or a Beefsteak and Burgundy Club never ever had an empty cellar.
> **BERNIE STEPHENS**

mouth, through the wine and food clubs … It became a very, very popular drink, complementing food in particular'.

These two worlds—the wine promoters and the wine-drinking public—intersected in the mid 1960s in spectacular fashion when Len Evans and Frank Margan swept through Renmark, in South Australia's Riverland, on a Wine Bureau trip. Frank sets the scene:

We were in Angoves, talking about the usual things, and one of the Angoves people said, 'We've got a very strong wine culture around here, actually. We've got a Wine and Food Society and it's very strong. We've got a wonderful cellar in the [local] hotel.' I was looking at Len out of the corner of my eye and he was looking at me. So we cut that interview fairly short and scarpered, straight down to the pub, to this gentleman who was dressed in a suit, actually. He looked like something out of Pickwick. 'Hear you've got some good wines here.' 'Yes, I have. Why? Are you interested?' 'Yes, could we have a look?' He took us down into the cellar and he was pointing out rows of half bottles of Maurice O'Shea Semillon, marked Riesling, of course. He said, 'They've been through three floods.' Oh, shit! Just the same, it's Maurice O'Shea wine and there's stacks of it. And the old little barrel labels of Elliotts wines. And so on and so on and so on. So we said, 'We'd like to buy it.' 'Oh, would you? I've been trying to get rid of it.'

Len continues the story:

I can remember this bloke standing at the counter of this closed bar with a ledger in front of him, and he said, 'Well, we'll start off with the '51 Mildara. We're happy to sell you any of these wines at cost price because we want to get rid of them. They're a liability. They don't sell and they're only sold to the Wine and Food Society Renmark.' They, stupidly, wouldn't buy. I mean, why they didn't buy the lot and have done with it, that was their problem. And he said, 'Seventeen cents a bottle. There's three dozen of that.' And we said, 'Yes, we'd like that. That would be wonderful.' And he said, 'The '52 has gone up in price. That's nineteen cents.' And so it went on. And even though they might've had it for twelve years, we still got it at the cost price—the book price. They wanted to get them off their books. I can remember there was a dozen '52 Wynns Coonawarra Cabernet standing up in a corner. I said, 'How long has that been standing up like that?' And he said, 'Oh, forever.' I said, 'That'll be no good.' He said, 'No, you can have that.' So it went on.

By the time they got back to Sydney, says Frank, the Wine and Food Society had discovered the 'theft' of their cellar, and sent a terse note: 'Do not come back to Renmark. You will be tarred and feathered.'

All the talk about wine in the press and on radio, combined with an increasing number of food and wine club lunches and dinners, inspired plenty of curiosity. People wanted to know where their wine came from, and began travelling to their closest vineyard area to find out. As a result, more and more wineries opened their cellar doors to this new wave of visitors. Where once the concept of selling direct to the public might have been nothing more than a winemaker in dirty overalls opening a bottle on an upturned barrel in the corner of the shed—and that's if the unannounced visitor had been lucky enough to catch the winemaker on his lunch break—now wineries started to pay more and more attention to the hospitality they offered.

Mickie Clifford (née Potts) remembers how the cellar door trade began to build at her family's Bleasdale winery at Langhorne Creek in the 1960s. The Potts family had been making wine in the region since 1850, but most was sold off in bulk to other wineries. The practice of bottling wine under their own label and selling it at the cellar door was a relatively new concept, but Mickie was clearly a natural salesperson and promoter. Here she re-enacts her routine:

'Oh, hullo. Good afternoon. Do come in. We have our wines set out on the table. You can help yourself to them but make sure that you can walk out by the time you go. And we have pictures.' [You would] soon tell if they're interested or not. If they were, you'd just go a bit further and tell them about the history and all that sort of stuff. If they were not, you'd just pass on the way and let them do what they wanted. Then they tried the wines. I've met people over there—awfully highbrow people—that really liked to show their knowledge on wine. You might get a couple of men there, and they'd stand inside of the table to help

themselves and all that, and there they were talking, 'Oh, no, the colour's not right. Peppery flavour,' and this sort of stuff. And I thought, oh, they're happy. Let them go. Didn't need any help from me whatsoever, so I let them go. And then, 'Thank you,' and they'd walk out after about two hours of talking about the wine. Just showing their knowledge.

Mickie recalls telling other visitors about the huge red gum press:

I told them about how they built it, when it was last used, and the boiler out the other side. I told them a lot about the history, and I'm very proud of it. And they'd listen. And the more you told them, the more they wanted to hear. But then if somebody didn't want to hear, they'd go back to the tasting and that was it. That's all right. Quite all right. Everybody's not the same. But I'm very keen on the history.

In an effort to attract even more visitors, and encourage them to stay longer, some regions established new events and festivals. Rutherglen held its first festival in 1967 and, according to Colin Campbell, its success took everyone a little by surprise: 'I guess it changed the whole nature of cellar door visits,' says Colin. 'The whole area changed very, very quickly. At that stage we didn't have any sort of sales area to sell our wine from, and very quickly we had to build a little shop at the front.'

Bill Chambers agrees, saying that the festival tapped a well of curiosity that was deeper than the winemakers realised. 'A lot of family groups came up. And [the festival] was fairly simple. It wasn't terribly expensive. So it was a hit,

really. Much more of a hit than we thought it was going to be.' Colin Campbell describes this period of the late 1960s, with estate-bottling, cellar door sales and the festival, as a new era for Rutherglen: 'The word "marketing" started suddenly to mean something to us.'

The popularity of this new phenomenon—wine tourism—grew during the 1970s and 1980s. And as it grew, winemakers came to learn that people who travelled to their region weren't only interested in wine. They were also attracted to other aspects of a civilised life such as fine food and music.

One of the first wineries to capitalise on this potential was Huntington Estate, in Mudgee. Bob Roberts found by accident that his winery was, acoustically, a great venue for musical events:

We were having a staff Christmas party in the winery and a fellow walked in. He was a music teacher and lived in Mudgee and he was going to teach Susie [Roberts, Bob's daughter] the clarinet. He had his clarinet with him and he played the slow movement of the Mozart clarinet concerto as he walked around the winery. It was so incredible that, with his help, we decided to put a concert on. That [grew] into the Huntington Music Festival, which ... gained international recognition.

The fledgling Margaret River region in Western Australia became home to another event in 1985 that married music and wine, when Denis and Tricia Horgan held the first Leeuwin Estate Concert—an event that almost didn't happen, according to Tricia:

We [had] a rather beautiful stand of karri trees that surrounded the open space between the winery and the creek. And we'd always looked at this very beautiful natural amphitheatre and thought it would be wonderful to have performing arts happening here. So we contacted the West Australian Symphony Orchestra and suggested that they might like to come down and do a concert on our front lawn. And they said at the time ... 'We're a serious orchestra. We don't play in the bush.' Never came. We approached the Opera Company and said, 'Well, come down and have a look'. They came down, clapped their hands and said, 'Good acoustics down here,' but never came back with a proposal ... One day the then-director of the Festival of Perth, [who had] made an approach to the London Philharmonic [Orchestra] but couldn't make the figures go round, [was] going up and down St George's Terrace saying to the local businesspeople, 'How about underwriting this?' [When he got to] Denis' office, [Denis] quickly said, 'Well, I wouldn't do it unless they play in my vineyard' ... A couple of days later he came back and he said, 'Well, there was stunned silence on the end of the phone in London when I said that to get this funding you have to go down 300 kilometres

Opposite: The annual Leeuwin Estate Concert series, held in the grounds of the Estate

Above: Rutherglen wine festival, 1970

south of Perth and play in somebody's vineyard, but they're really keen to come so, yes, they'll do it.' And we said, 'Oh, how do we make this work?' So we started asking a few friends, 'If we had the London Philharmonic play on our front lawn, how many people do you think we'd get?' One friend came back to us and said, 'I've been sent by your other friends. Don't shoot the messenger but we think you're absolutely mad. Put up the money and don't have them because you'll be written up as the absolute eccentric businessman who tried to put on a concert on his front lawn.'

The Horgans ignored this advice and managed to convince the board of Leeuwin it was not only a good idea, but an idea that would work. And they were right: 'It just went mad,' says Tricia. 'Thousands had decided that they were coming to this thing and we had no idea how many people you could get on the lawn.'

After arriving with a bang, the annual Leeuwin Estate Concert went on to become a huge cultural event that helped to cement Margaret River's reputation as an especially sophisticated winegrowing district.

THE HISTORY OF AUSTRALIAN WINE

As well as learning how to attract visitors to their region by putting on festivals, concerts and other events, winemakers learned that sometimes it's worthwhile taking the wines to the customers in the form of trade tastings and travelling exhibitions.

In 1981, Betty Quick from Forest Hill vineyard was one of a small group from the Great Southern region in Western Australia who travelled to Melbourne for one of these trade events, Wine Expo. Betty's description of the comments she received during the tasting demonstrate how much of a novelty Western Australian wine was in the eastern states, even in the early 1980s, and how important face-to-face marketing was.

You'd have thought from the people coming through [at the Wine Expo] that we really came from somewhere different, almost to the stage of them asking 'Did we have kangaroos jumping down the main street of Perth?' And people would say that when the road's bituminised we'll come over and see you. I thought, oh, yes, I've heard that before. But it was surprising, in the cellar years later, that someone had come in and they'd say, 'Oh, I met you in Melbourne. Told you I was coming' … Probably at that stage I felt that we sold more tourism than we did wine, because people didn't know anything much about Western Australia. The great percentage had never come to Western Australia so this was a catalyst. I must admit we used this with the government later on to get more funding: that it wasn't just the wine we were selling, we were selling the state as well.

Merv Lange was another Great Southern winemaker on that trip to Melbourne. Like Betty, Merv was an ex-farmer who had made the transition to wine, and visiting the Big Smoke was full of adventure:

I'll never forget the first time that we started marketing wine outside of WA … Jude and myself were there and Tony Smith from Plantagenet, Michael Goundrey, and Betty from Forest Hill. Betty in Melbourne! I mean, we were staying in this hotel out at St Kilda. It was funny. It was right where all the brothels used to be. Anyway, at the time, all the girls in this one area used to sit on this big stone fence and wait for the customers. And of course we never knew. Course, there's Bet sitting there and waiting for us. And she's sitting there, boots and all, and couldn't work out why all these blokes are coming up to be so friendly to her. Bet was so naive that she never ever worked it out … I'll never forget that night. We got back from the city in a taxi and we were talking about it. The taxi driver was that rapt in what we were talking about that he turned his meter off and said, 'Look, I'm going to drive you mob around for fifteen minutes and show you some real sights.' It was a classic.

Following pages: Mount Mary vineyard in the Yarra Valley

CHAPTER 8

BOOM AND BUST

The business of Australian wine

The industry is now more sophisticated. It's very much more industry oriented. Before, it was farming people making wine … But now it really is big business.

ROGER MACMAHON

The usual metaphor trundled out to describe the volatile nature of the Australian wine business is that it is a 'rollercoaster ride'. This is certainly an image that must resonate with today's generation of grape-growers, winemakers, retailers and shareholders: in the last decade the wine industry has plummeted from a lofty peak of unprecedented export growth and optimism to the depths of oversupply, financial turmoil and despair. Luna Park is a gentle Sunday drive by comparison.

Older hands in the game know, however, that the current challenges are nothing new. There have been slumps before. There have been good times before. And the boom and bust cycle is sure to keep repeating long into the future. Veteran players also observe that, just as the rollercoaster ride always returns to the beginning—and starts all over again—so has the Australian wine industry come full circle in many ways from where it began at the beginning of the twentieth century.

Back then, families dominated the wine landscape: almost all the big companies that are now household names—Penfolds, Seppelt, Hardys, Orlando—were family-owned. Co-operative wineries, established by growers, were the next development, followed by a series of takeovers, mergers and acquisitions. Massive consolidation then left the industry dramatically polarised, with a handful of very large publicly listed companies down on one side of the see-saw and thousands of very small family-owned companies hanging on for dear life up the other end. In the period since the interviews for this book were recorded, that balance has

Opposite: Corporate headquarters, Yalumba Perth office, 1960

started to shift, with the giant corporates fracturing and the family-owned companies taking a more important role. The industry, in other words, looks like heading back to where it all began.

In the beginning: a family affair

Jack Babidge's family cooperage had been making barrels for South Australian wineries for years when he joined the firm in the mid 1930s. Back then, says Jack, the wine industry was 'a happy association. It was friendship more than anything. You made friends, and then business followed along ... right throughout the industry'.

Alex Johnston of Pirramimma winery explains how the family networks operated in the 1930s. Alex's mother's best friend was Elsie Wigan, who had married Ron Haselgrove, manager of the Mildura Wine Company. 'Ron,' says Alex, 'realised that he needed better base material for making his flor sherry ... So he suggested to my father that Pirramimma should grow some pedro and palomino and he would buy the base wine, which he did.'

Then, as now, a major advantage of family ownership is the ability it gives

companies to think long term and re-invest rather than be driven by annual returns. Mark Tummel's recollection of the Barossa Pearl phenomenon at the Gramp family–owned Orlando in the 1950s is a perfect illustration:

Barossa Pearl … brought some cash flow to the Gramp family because the wine industry has always been a very capital-intensive industry. To Colin [Gramp]'s credit he could convince other members of the family to spend some money and I'm sure they spent money rather than have dividends … It was spent on improving the business.

Grower vs. winery: a precarious relationship

The strong sense of family that existed within the wine companies also traditionally extended to relations between the wineries and the growers who supplied the grapes. The Barossa ritual of growers joining winemaker Peter Lehmann in the weighbridge for a *schluck* and a *schnitte*—a glass of port and a slice of sausage—after delivering their grapes during vintage isn't just some folksy ideal; it was the way that business was done: with a handshake and a hearty toast.

Large companies such as Orlando attempted to maintain this spirit even though they dealt with more than 500 growers across Australia. Neil Wilkinson was vineyard manager for Orlando in the 1960s:

We spent a lot of time out in the vineyards with growers. The grower liaison side of it became quite a big operation … If a grower came to us and wanted to know what varieties to plant, we would make a suggestion if we felt confident about the industry. It wasn't so much an advisory service, it was a liaison service, and by selecting our growers we were pretty sure of our quality.

I was able to develop a good rapport with them. They knew me, they knew our family, they knew where our property was and, you know, they knew that we were people who you could rely on.

As the industry grew, however, and the companies became more corporate and less personal, it became harder to maintain the friendship and sense of obligation. In some of the tough years of the early 1960s, when there were too many grapes on the vine and too much wine sitting in the cellars, some wineries reneged on their contracts with the growers, which resulted in bitter acrimony.

This tension between growers and wineries—especially in regions such as the Barossa and the Riverland, both characterised by an inherently inequitable situation where many small-scale farmers supply a few large-scale winemakers—has become a recurring theme in the ensuing decades. The sense of alienation and mistrust that both sides have, at times, felt towards each other has been at the heart of many of the problems that continue to trouble the industry.

One of the darkest chapters in the saga of grower/winemaker relations came in 1978—but it resulted in the formation of one of Australia's brightest winemaking companies.

Peter Lehmann was the well-ensconced, much-loved winemaker at Saltram, then owned by the English pastoral company Dalgety. As usual, the winemaker had arranged to buy grapes from his loyal growers with a handshake deal. But, remembers Peter, Dalgety was feeling the pressure of the downturn in the wine industry and had other ideas:

I was just one day opening the mail and there was a letter from the company secretary advising me not to buy any grapes from the Barossa growers for the coming vintage. I couldn't believe my bloody eyes. I thought a phone call and discussion [would have been more appropriate]. But this just came out of the blue. So I got hot on the phone and tried every trick in the trade. And they just said that, no, you've got to send [out letters to the growers]. And I said, 'I'm not sending out any letters.' So [they] said, 'Well, we'll send them out.' They just sent

Above: Penfolds board meeting, 1972

out a letter to all the growers saying that regrettably we won't be able to take any of your grapes for the 1978 vintage, which left me in a hell of a position—because where was this trust? This handshake deal?

Peter's response, famously, was to form his own company and buy the grapes himself, borrowing way beyond his means. And ironically, as soon as he started processing the grapes, Dalgety realised they did need to make some wine after all. 'So they became our second-biggest customer,' says Peter. 'It was that bloody ludicrous.'

Initially, Peter Lehmann envisaged his company would become a bulk supplier to the industry, supporting those growers left in the lurch by the big corporates.

[But] by 1982, people to whom I was expecting to be selling in bulk were out there selling [in] bulk themselves. And we realised that the only possible way we'd survive was for us to go into what I call the glass jungle—that is, the bottle market ... So that's how [the] Peter Lehmann [name] came to appear on the labels.

The rise and fall of the co-ops

Some grape-growers had responded to earlier downturns by forming co-operatives, notably in wine regions along the Murray River where the new soldier settlement vineyards had fuelled an export boom in the 1920s and 1930s. In the 1950s and 1960s, these co-ops were able to supply increasing amounts of the newly popular table wines in bulk to wineries, which would bottle them under their own labels. The co-ops were initially assisted financially by loans from the State Bank, with tax-deductible repayments. But by the 1980s, increased corporatisation and competition made it difficult for the co-operative model to survive.

In the early 1980s, Kaiser Stuhl was one of the biggest co-ops—it had already merged with the Waikerie and Clarevale co-ops—but, according to managing director Keith Smith, it was struggling:

It was apparent that we would never be able to challenge the big boys, and grow. Maybe one day we might have been able to do a management buyout but they weren't even heard of in those days. So we looked around for a partner and the most obvious partner was right next door. At Penfolds. And I approached John Spalvins and said, 'Look, I think the shareholders would be willing to sell this business provided that their security was assured with long-term grape contracts and they get a reasonable price for their shares today.' And that happened.

Two of the other big co-ops, Berri and Renmano, decided that they would strengthen their positions by merging. John Pendrigh was the executive at Berri Estates who oversaw the merger and took the new combined entity on a new path:

So we put those two together and became consolidated co-operative wineries and started then to look seriously at developing our own brands, particularly the Chairman's Selection brand that Renmano had put together. And it went quite well from thereon in … [but] the co-operative structure was no longer serving our best interests as it was, or the best interests of the shareholders. It was time that we restructured the organisation to give us an opportunity to go into the market and acquire companies that had brands that were acceptable, and expand. We did this, and we completely restructured the company in 1988. The cooperative then became the supply company and the holder of the shares in the new publicly unlisted company called BRL.

And BRL, of course, would go on to buy the old family firm Hardys, resulting in one of the country's largest wine companies.

The acquisition trail: takeovers and mergers

A run of large-scale acquisitions had kicked off in 1961, when Lindemans purchased Leo Buring in the Barossa Valley and The Distillers Company, a UK drinks business, purchased Tolley, Scott and Tolley. Neither was all that unusual: there is a long tradition of wine companies both here and in the UK buying and selling other Australian wine companies. But these two acquisitions in 1961 sparked a frenzy of winery purchases by non-wine companies, many of them based overseas. In 1963, the large national grocer Crooks National Holdings bought Woodley Wines; in 1966, Seager Evans (UK) bought Tulloch in the Hunter Valley, and Reed Paper (UK) bought Glenloth, near Reynella, in South Australia; in 1969, Reed bought Tulloch and a year later took over McLaren Vale Wines and Ryecroft, while Reckitt and Coleman purchased Morris Wines at Rutherglen, and Allied Vintners bought Seaview and Glenloth from Reed.

These acquisitions and changes changed forever the structure of the Australian wine industry and deeply challenged the tradition of family and co-operative ownership. For some observers, international takeovers have been almost universal failures: Wolf Blass points out that, apart from Pernod Ricard (owners of Orlando and Jacob's Creek), not one overseas company has been able to run a wine business in Australia successfully. But for others, there was an upside to being taken over. According to Mick Morris of Morris Wines, the sale to Reckitt and Coleman breathed new life into the business—although he had to dig his heels in to get his way:

We sold out … not because we had to financially, but Uncle Fred wanted to do his own thing and we didn't have enough money to buy him out. We thought for the sake of family harmony we'd put the place on the market and if we got a price that was satisfactory we'd sell it. And that's what happened … I think [Reckitt and Coleman] thought when they bought us that they'd buy wine in and just expand it. That's not how the wine industry works … Part of the deal [was] that I became the winemaker. But I wouldn't sign anything. I said, 'Look, if you don't like me, you can sack me. And if I don't like the way that you run things, I'll leave.' I don't think we could've had a better company takeover. They managed the financial side, eventually taking over the marketing side, but we did our own thing as far as making the wine. With our stocks of old wine they used to say, 'Well, how much can we have this year?' rather than come in and say, 'Right, we're going to sell all your old stocks.' A lot of the earlier takeovers sold their stocks of old wine, but we were allowed to keep control of the old stock and gradually get rid of them. We were gradually replacing them so that we still had old stocks for blending. We kept making wine the traditional way.

I said, 'Look, if you don't like me, you can sack me. And if I don't like the way that you run things, I'll leave.'

MICK MORRIS

The acquisitions continued into the 1970s: Heinz bought the Stanley Wine Company, Philip Morris bought Lindemans, Reckitt and Coleman bought Orlando, Rothmans bought Reynella, Tooheys bought into Wynns. For Orlando winemaker Philip Laffer, it was an exciting and important time. 'Every one of those companies left behind it this enormous legacy of a colossal investment,' he says. 'The vineyard developments of Padthaway, wineries like Lindemans Karadoc, would never have happened without the ability of these large international companies to pour an awful lot of money in … They arrived at a time when the industry was just taking off and needed a lot of cash to be injected.'

Some of the bigger family-owned companies struggled to keep up with the levels of investment required to compete in this new, expanding market. As Ross Jenkins of Seppelt points out, the number of shareholders expanded within the family as the family grew, and many of them saw a better return in selling their shares, opening the company up to takeovers.

For Bill Hardy, the change of ownership came as a personal blow. He was in France, setting up a new winery, when Hardys decided to forego its private status, to bring in outside capital to merge and float. 'When I left [to go to France] we were a great old South Australian family company,' says Bill. 'When I came back we were a very new, young, listed public company … It absolutely devastated me at the time.'

By the time of the stock market crash and cripplingly high interest rates of the late 1980s, the international companies that had entered the industry so boldly over the previous two decades were beginning to feel the pinch. Reckitt and Coleman at Orlando was one example, as Perry Gunner recounts:

Most of those companies came to the same sort of conclusion about the same time … They started to look to what they could divest and where they could better use that money. Reckitt and Coleman came to the conclusion that a wine company in Australia was not the best thing they could invest in, that they should invest in household businesses … Their chief executive came out to Australia with the brief to sell the business. [They] found there was very little interest … So it was all looking a bit doom and gloom in the wine industry. However, we had started to export Jacob's Creek … 1987 was the first year that we actually had it in the market, having spent '86 getting someone interested. So there were a few signs … we felt pretty confident as management. And so, there was a management buyout.

Large Australian companies took advantage of the rapidly shifting business landscape and started buying the brands that the overseas investors were all too keen to sell. Wolf Blass, who had gone public with his eponymous wine company in

1984 but retained a majority share, remembers being in London when he heard the news that the South Australian Brewing Company had bought Lindemans and Penfolds:

I nearly fell over. That was 36 per cent [of the market]. I said, 'We'll go. We'll not survive. We're not surviving now. Being a public company we can't survive. When one company controls 36 per cent of the market, bloody hell, we're going to go.'

Wolf flew straight back to Australia, and approached Ross Wilson of SA Brewing, offering to buy one of his newly acquired brands. At the same time, Ray King of Mildara was making similar overtures. Wilson wasn't selling, though, so Wolf and Ray started talking to each other about a merger—despite some deep misgivings among Wolf's fellow directors:

My board took some convincing. But I said that I thought it was the best thing— for the best interest of the wine company and for the best interest of the shareholders. I was quite ready to move sideways. There's only one bloody bloke can be the chief executive. And Ray said, 'All right, I'm going to use you for export.' Then I was a major shareholder. Everybody said that it was a takeover. Couldn't have been a takeover, I was the biggest bloody shareholder.

Mass marketing and the new consumer

As with any industry, the people who are on the fringes—the suppliers rather than the producers—often have a more acute ability to see the bigger picture. Roger Macmahon's family company sold and manufactured corks in South Australia, and Roger believes the wave of rationalisation and consolidation that started in the 1980s brought a new professionalism to the wine business. 'The industry is now more sophisticated,' he says. 'It's very much more industry oriented. Before, it was farming people making wine … But now it really is big business. Even with a small winery they have to be pretty much on the ball to compete. And I think that's the main difference.'

Bernie Stephens says that while the takeovers were 'inevitable' and the corporatisation has been 'a bit sad … the industry has not really lost too much in character or characters … In fact, it's been good for the industry in the commercial sense, inasmuch as it provided that incentive, it provided the power that was able to put wine into the world markets'.

Guenter Prass makes a crucial observation that the arrival of the large corporate owners and their sophisticated marketing departments coincided with the growth of the merchants and their focus on discounting. 'This [was] really modern marketing of consumer goods,' says Guenter. 'The choice was to stay a cottage industry or develop into a modern beverage industry.'

It was a profound shift in the philosophy of how wine companies should be run—a fundamental challenge to the traditional production-driven model of the wine trade. As Orlando's Mark Tummel points out:

When Reckitt and Coleman bought Orlando … we had product managers appointed to handle portfolios of products within the total range and they were the people that dictated the styles. And they were the people who came to the winemakers and said, 'Hey! This is what we want.' And so we made according to what the marketer wanted, not what the winemakers wanted to put out there. And that was an enormous change. Because up till that time the winemakers dictated. They said, 'Here! This is an excellent wine. Go out and sell it, boys.' And when Reckitt and Coleman came in that was reversed completely … They put in very strong marketing teams, including product managers. I mean, [the] industry hadn't heard of product managers. So they put in product managers responsible for particular portfolios of the range, and they dictated what they wanted.

Opposite: Open wine displays changed the way consumers improved their wine knowledge

A HEADY MIX
Wine and politics

Throughout the twentieth century, various lobby groups, peak bodies and representative organisations have emerged in the wine industry, many formed as a response to external threats to the industry's prosperity and survival.

In 1918, for example, faced with a swing towards prohibition in Australia, a group of industry representatives including Dr Thomas Fiaschi, Eric Lindeman, Oscar Seppelt, Tom Hardy, Frank Penfold Hyland and Cuthbert Burgoyne—the old boys' wine trade network—formed the Federal Viticultural Council of Australia and successfully lobbied governments and the press until the prohibitionist cause subsided.[1]

In some cases, though, no amount of industry lobbying could stem the tide of government intervention. Adelaide's urban sprawl in the middle years of the century, for example, hastened by the State Government's compulsory acquisition of land, swallowed many famous old vineyards, including those owned by Tolley's Pedare, in the city's north-eastern outskirts. 'At one stage we had up to 400 acres [of vines] at Modbury, Tea Tree Gully and Hope Valley,' says Reg Tolley, invoking names that people today associate with Adelaide suburbia. 'The State Government took over a lot of that land, unfortunately ... It was dreadful. Yes, we tried to fight it. Well, we couldn't. They [the government] said, "We want the land."'

During the early 1960s, a surplus of grapes in South Australia forced many growers to pull up their vines, and led to a State Government Royal Commission into the wine industry. This parlous situation inspired some growers, such as Leo Pech in the

Barossa, to get involved politically and try to change things for the better. Along with others in the grape-growing community, Leo believed it was crucial to establish a vine selection society to not only improve the quality of both planting decisions and planting material, but to enhance relationships with the wineries—the companies that bought the grapes:

Without the support of, in particular, Kaiser Stuhl, Yalumba, Orlando, Penfolds, Seppelt and Chateau Yaldara, we would not have been able to achieve what we did achieve in such a short period ... [We] didn't have the financial ability. We needed winemaker support. And without the support from the winemakers we would not have achieved what we were able to. That was the concept behind setting up a vine selection society, which was actually formed in 1965.

Many winemakers point to the tax changes introduced by the Whitlam government in 1973 as being a pivotal point in the Australian wine story. Ray Beckwith explains the implications of the abolition of Section 31A of the Taxation Act:

[Before the change] winemakers [had been] permitted for taxation purposes to bring the wine into their books at nominal value, just as the farmers did with the sheep at a nominal rate ... tax would be collected when the wine, or the animals, were sold. When the profit was made. But then, with this change, the wine had to be brought into accounting at cost, or market value, whichever was the lesser. And, of course, this created some difficulties because it was an extra impost. Another case of shifting the goalposts, as it were.

Winemakers were furious when they heard about the abolition of section 31A. Frank Devine, managing director at Wynns and president of the Australian Wine and Brandy Producers Association at the time, was given a golden opportunity to vent his spleen when he ran into Gough Whitlam in an Adelaide hotel. Frank suggested that the government should phase in the changes rather then bring them in suddenly. But Whitlam was having none of it:

'Oh, no, we're not going to do that,' [he said]. We had quite an argument. There'd been a big fire [at one of the wineries] and then he said to me, 'That's what you bloody-well ought to do, have a couple more fires,' and stalked off. I'd got his knickers in a knot because what I was saying was quite practicable … He didn't listen to me, for what it's worth.

The scars of this time still linger. Don McWilliam describes the industry's disagreement with the government as the 'Donnybrook of all Donnybrooks', and says he was tempted to fill a few road tankers up with wine, take them down to Canberra and pump the value of the wine into the cellars of Parliament House in protest. McLaren Vale winemaker Jim Ingoldby is even more blunt: 'I always say the two big disasters in my life were World War II and Gough Whitlam. In that order.'

Above: Douglas Anthony (right), then Federal Minister for Primary Industry, presenting Penfolds winemaker Don Ditter with a trophy at the Sydney Wine Show in the late 1960s

A major instance of government intervention in the wine industry at this time was the South Australian state-sponsored vine-pull scheme that was introduced in 1985 to address the oversupply of (mostly red) grapes.

'The vine-pull scheme was administered by the Department of Agriculture with no parameters and no criteria,' remembers viticulturist Di Davidson.

[The government offered growers] $3000 a hectare to pull [their vines] out. A grower was doing really well to net $1500 a hectare, or even $1000 a hectare [from selling grapes]. So those on the bones of their bum just said, 'Three thousand dollars? Thank you.' [But] the department had no criteria at all; that was apparent to any of us watching what happened. [No-one had thought] about what variety should and shouldn't come out in what location ... They were very hard years and seeing those heaps of vines [was] terrible ... I met so many people who were struggling so badly—I guess from about '81 to '85 would have to be the really low point for the production side of the industry.

Another blow in the 1980s was the introduction of a tax on retail wine sales. While the industry found it difficult to adapt to this impost, it inspired more unification, to fight the common enemy of government. As Perry Gunner says, 'It started to galvanise the industry, at least about one issue, and that was taxation.'

According to John Pendrigh of the Berri Renmano co-op, by this time the Australian Wine and Brandy Producers Association—the industry's main body—had become a 'bull-pit for fighting. There was no consensus of opinion as to where the industry should go, how it should, in fact, address itself to all the issues that were facing it'. Indeed, Pendrigh felt so disillusioned that his company left the association and began lobbying separately for the co-ops.

At the same time, frustrated by the big companies' domination of the AWBPA and its 'laissez-faire [approach to] industry, where dog ate dog', Brian Croser established the Winemakers' Forum for small producers. 'The opportunity was becoming very obvious for the Australian wine industry in premium wine,' says Brian. '[So] John Pendrigh and I got together [and] we forced the Wine and Brandy Producers Association basically into accepting that it

was a three-way division of power with government and we would all go together.'

This three-pronged group formalised itself into the Federation of Australian Winemakers' Associations (FAWA), which eventually became the Winemakers' Federation of Australia in 1990.

'It's really from that point that the industry started to make some progress in its export markets,' says John Pendrigh. 'We revamped our own organisation so that we had a single voice in industry and we worked cooperatively together, particularly in our export markets ... Our own domestic market wasn't growing fast enough and we didn't have the strength to really get our prices where they should be.'

Above: Prime Minister John Howard celebrating with Wolf Blass the release of the historical fourth Jimmy Watson trophy winner at a fundraising event

Right: Govenor-General Sir Zelman Cowan visits Yalumba, 1979

Opposite: The Duke of Edinburgh visits Yalumba, 1974

CHAPTER 9

FROM EMPIRE PORT TO YELLOW TAIL

Selling Australian wine overseas

Back in 1973, I was told that there's no hope for the Australian wine industry in exports. We have no reputation. We're on the wrong side of the world.

PERRY GUNNER

Back in the late nineteenth century, Hubert de Castella's book about his experiences as a gentleman vigneron in Victoria's Yarra Valley, *John Bull's Vineyard*, issued a call to arms for Australia to become the pre-eminent wine supplier to the British Empire.

The wines that de Castella had in mind were light, dry table wines of the type that his St Huberts vineyard and many other nineteenth-century Victorian properties produced with such panache. These table wines did not, sadly, catch on at the time, either with local drinkers or, indeed, with the denizens of old John Bull.

But a very thirsty market did develop in the United Kingdom for Australian wines of the strong, bold, *fortified* kind, such as the aptly named Empire Port. Indeed, by the 1930s, Australian wine exports to the 'old country' were on a par with Britain's veteran traditional suppliers, Portugal, Spain and France; in fact, in some years, such as 1933 and 1938, Australia shipped more wine to England than either the French or the Spanish.

During the 1930s Yalumba was doing a roaring trade to the UK, regularly exporting 1000 hogsheads at a time. And the vast majority of this wine was fortified and sweet—port, sherry and madeira: between 1936 and 1937, Yalumba shipped no fewer than 3631 hogsheads, of which just 1.7 per cent was dry table wine.[1]

This vibrant colonial trade even managed to struggle through the economic

downturn of the 1930s, and kept many wineries and vineyards afloat during tough times. In the late 1930s, Ben Chaffey started work at South Australia's Emu Wine Company, one of the biggest and most important exporters. Chaffey remembers Emu shipping wine to Canada, Ireland, England, India, Java and Borneo, 'to wherever there were red spots'—or outposts of the old British Empire—on the map:

The Emu Wine Company virtually kept lots and lots of little wineries all around South Australia solvent, particularly in the southern area, and each year after vintage, we'd buy their wine. They'd bring samples in and my job was to make up blends in the laboratory. Of course, these had to be standardised in colour and strength and character, and so on, to be sent to England year after year. And, of course, we made a hell of a lot of sweet wine blends by buying from Angoves and Berri. Very often we'd have it sent direct from Mildura, Angoves, Berri. Others, like Waikerie, occasionally. Also, we had a railway siding built into the winery at Morphett Vale. We'd have stuff trucked straight down and we had facilities for emptying hogsheads straight in. Roll them off the trucks and down under a hole in the floor and then they'd pump it away. We'd make 50-odd thousand gallon blends on order.

By the time World War II erupted in 1939, Australia was exporting 25 per cent of its annual wine production. But the war quickly took its toll on this success story, and wine exports slumped and then stagnated for decades, with just a small, steady trickle flowing out of the country.

The middle years: exports in decline

During the 1950s and 1960s, sluggish exports became the norm for many in the Australian wine industry, so much so that by the 1970s, when a rise in domestic consumption and general interest in wine prompted some of the new wave of entrepreneurs to think about exploring overseas markets, they were met with a wall of stony indifference. As Rosemount's Chris Hancock puts it, for many overseas buyers, 'Australian wine was steeped in a tradition of failure.'

Perry Gunner remembers coming up against this attitude at the time:

When I raised the issue of exports in my first week at Orlando back in 1973, I was told that there's no hope for the Australian wine industry in exports. We have no reputation. We're on the wrong side of the world and we could never produce it as well, or as cheaply, as the Europeans, and there was an absolute defeatist attitude in the business and, I think, in the industry about what we could do in the export arena.

Above left: Australian Wine and
Food Festival, Tokyo, 1969

Bruce Tyrrell tells a story of his early days trying to sell wines in the United
States, and being thrown out of the best liquor store in Manhattan:

I'd gone in [and introduced myself]: 'Bruce Tyrrell, Tyrrell's Wines. We're [from]
the emerging wine nation of the world.' And the guy just turned his back and
walked away. And so I kept following him around the shop with the story. And he
turned around to me and he said, 'Look, they don't make wine in Australia … So
go away.' I said, 'I'll see you next year.' And he said, 'Don't ever walk in the door
again.' Took seven years, [but] we got in there.

Driven by Ross Brown, Brown Brothers began their, eventually successful, foray
into export in the early 1970s. But it wasn't easy at first. 'Ross went off-shore
looking for markets in the UK,' remembers John Brown. '[It was] very difficult
to get anybody to take on a new brand when nobody knows it, but he managed
to convince a few people to put the product on the shelf.'

Grant Burge recalls receiving a cold reaction from the international wine
industry in the 1970s: 'Not only did they not want our wine, they didn't even
want to taste it,' he says. But, rather than deterring him, the experience made him
'more determined that Australian wine had a real future, not only in Australia but
in an export sense'.

Robert Hill Smith of Yalumba returned from a trip to Europe in 1978, also seeing opportunity in adversity:

[That trip] was pivotal, absolutely, not only [in] building my knowledge and respect for the tradition of wine in a European context, but … from a business perspective it helped me understand that Australia *had* to have a role in the international wine trade … Historically, this country has been and had to be, as an island continent, a country of traders. But, in the wine industry I don't think my generation at the time respected how important international sales had been to the Australian wine industry. Nor did they probably comprehend how important they could be in the future. When I came back in '79 and, I think, saw that this country was, in a wine sense, in a pretty parlous state, my view was to get international or get out. I suppose I didn't necessarily describe it that way at the time, but I did see a terrific future.

The early 1980s: the phoenix begins to stir

Together with Brown Brothers, one of the first Australian wine brands to really crack the UK market in the 1980s was Rosemount, with a peachy-golden chardonnay sporting a distinctive yellow diamond-shaped label. With the 1983 London Wine Trade Fair looming, Rosemount's Chris Hancock hit upon the idea of a media tasting at Lord's cricket ground to coincide with a Middlesex vs. Surrey match:

Above: Chris Hancock

These were the days of 'Beefy' Botham and Graham Gooch and Geoffrey Boycott … They were giving us a thrashing all the time, so the English were very pleased with themselves about cricket. And the deal was basically that, look, even if [the trade] didn't want any of the wines, they would come and see this annual [match] … So we sent out sixty invitations and I thought that if we got half of them that wasn't bad. Thirty people would be good. [But then] I got up in the morning and looked out of the window and it is pissing down with rain. I mean, it is pouring with rain. Get out to Lord's, and the cricket's been cancelled. Along the low side of Lord's there's that much bloody water. So that's the end of that [I thought]. There's no cricket, so nobody's going to come … [But] we got sixty-three people out of sixty invitations! Just extraordinary. Curiosity brought them out. They were terribly impressed. And Hugh Johnson was there [among others]. Not the modern names: all of the great old English wine writers and all that sort of thing, they all turned up. Had lunch. Had a lovely day. Why did they come? Oh, it was such a wet day that it was a good thing to do. Funny, eh? So we had a huge success with the launch.

Chris Hancock also got to know Oz Clarke, one of the up-and-coming UK wine writers, who was also a professional actor, singing in *Evita* on Shaftesbury Avenue. In Oz's dressing room after the show, Chris was surprised to find a cupboard full of Wynns wines from Coonawarra. As it turned out, says Chris, Oz described himself as 'an Australian nut. I love the stuff'.

A couple of days later, the London Wine Trade Fair had begun and Chris was staying in the West End. A colleague phoned and excitedly told him that Rosemount had just got distribution in Peter Dominic's, the leading off-premise chain in those days.

He said, 'Go and have a look in Peter Dominic's window in Orange Street, just off Haymarket, before you come out to the Wine Trade Fair.' So I did. The window was full of bloody Rosemount chardonnay. I was so excited I nearly wet myself. It was just wonderful. That gave us huge confidence. And off we went … We had no idea. There was no market. We had to make the market.

John Pendrigh, who at the time was CEO of the Berri Renmano co-operative, remembers an equally enthusiastic—if slightly different—reception at a wine fair in Bristol the same year:

[The trade fair] was held on the old wharves in Bristol. And it was a year in which it was a heat wave in Britain and it was so hot that the tar macadam on the road was actually melting. It was blistering. And, of course, in this tin shed—the world's wines were there and we were all in this—there was no refrigeration. There was no air-conditioning. There was nothing. [But we had] a new wine cooling system … and we were mobbed because we had these 2 litre flagons of Fruity Gordo Moselle, which is fairly alcoholic, very, very tasty, and we could actually pump it cool through this thing. And, of course, people were drinking it like beer and they were just absolutely plastered … The damage that Fruity Gordo Moselle did to the Bristol population, you won't believe! It was very popular because it was cold and it was wet. It was very hot weather. In fact, I think we wiped out the whole of the Welsh rugby team, who also happened to be there.

John Pendrigh, wearing his other, Wine and Brandy Producers Association board-member hat, was also one of the people responsible in the late 1980s for setting up a London office, as part of the Australian Trade Commission, to promote the country's wines in the burgeoning export market. The first person appointed to run this office was the enthusiastic and energetic northerner, Hazel Murphy, who would do more than almost anyone to build Australia's image in the UK as a quality wine-producing nation. 'She did a great job for the industry,' says John Pendrigh. 'The fact that we had our own person there and that we funded her office through the Wine and Brandy Corporation, really gave us that constant presence in the UK market, just at a time when all the companies had suddenly realised that here was an opportunity.'

A perfect storm: the banana republic, Masters of Wine and Chernobyl

Intrigued by the energy, the sense of fun and the sheer can-do attitude of the Australian winemakers who made their mark in the UK in the early 1980s, in 1985 a group of British Masters of Wine travelled Down Under for a tour of Australian wine regions. The Institute of Masters of Wine is a prestigious and elite group of wine professionals—merchants, media, vignerons—that wields enormous influence in the global trade. The tour was organised by Hazel Murphy, who believed that it would be good for the MWs to see for themselves what was going on. According to Perry Gunner of Orlando, it was a pivotal visit:

They could not believe what they saw. I was with them at Rowland Flat—it was towards the end of their visit—and they just were in awe of the quality of the wines we were producing, at the price we could afford to sell them. They just could not believe that such a country existed. And so they went back, talking up the Australian wine industry like you couldn't believe.

Winemaker Pam Dunsford remembers the MWs visiting the Glenloth winery. They were particularly impressed with the quality of the fruit—'that bottled sunshine flavour'; they loved being able to taste some classic older Australian wines from the 1960s, and they couldn't believe the low prices of the wines.

I remember that there was a function held at Reynell's homestead for the MWs. Greg Trott [of Wirra Wirra] organised it. And I thought that I was going to a free lunch but, of course, there's nothing free in the wine industry. And, at the end of that, Jancis Robinson [the British MW and wine writer] had a film crew … saying, 'Okay, what's Australia, and why is it different?' And then that went straight back to the UK and was broadcast everywhere … It was *the* beginning.

The MW trip was a crucial factor in the export renaissance in the mid 1980s. But there were other, equally important, elements to the story. For a start, as Perry Gunner points out, there was a surplus of wine in Australia. Orlando had been planting quite a bit of chardonnay and Perry remembers Mark Tummel, the chief winemaker, warning him in the early 1980s: 'You guys will never be able to sell all the chardonnay that's going into the ground.' He was right, of course, and it forced Orlando and others to look elsewhere.

They just could not believe that such a country existed. And so they went back, talking up the Australian wine industry like you wouldn't believe.
PERRY GUNNER

Luckily, as Guenter Prass explains, history conspired to encourage 'elsewhere'—the rest of the world—suddenly to look at Australia with fresh eyes:

[Prime Minister Paul] Keating's remark about Australia being a banana republic lowered the exchange rate from 85 cents to the US dollar to 56 cents to the US dollar. [So] Australia was, overnight, price competitive. The Chernobyl nuclear disaster happened and overnight all European vineyards were in doubt of having been affected by the nuclear cloud. [But] Australia was far away: a 'green' country, a safe country. A number of countries, Canada and Nordic countries, applied trade restrictions to the import of goods from South Africa because of the apartheid policies of the South African government. [But] Australia was politically stable.

'There'd been a lot of attempts at exporting Australian wine prior to the '80s,' says Phil Laffer. 'All had failed because it was seen as an exercise of quitting what we didn't want. [Then] with [companies] attempting in the '80s to actually sell branded Australian wine overseas, suddenly people realised that we had something very special in Australia, in terms of style and our ability to produce high-quality, affordable wines.'

The 1990s: export shifts into overdrive; the industry develops a 'strategy'

When Chris Hancock was pouring Rosemount chardonnay at Lord's in 1983, Australia's annual wine exports were about 11 million litres, worth around $13 million. Ten years later, that had grown to 125 million litres, worth $370 million. And it showed no sign of stopping during the following decade: by 2003 the annual export of 580 million litres of Australian wine was worth $2.5 billion.[2] (It's worth pointing out here that most of the interviews quoted in this book were recorded around this time, in the early 2000s, during the fat years of the export boom, well before oversupply, the GFC and a stronger Aussie dollar put a big, wet dampener on things.)

Throughout the 1990s, the world couldn't get enough of Australian wines. They offered great value for money. Australia boasted some strong brands. And, most of all, the wines delivered oodles of fruity, sunshiny flavour: as Wolf Blass puts it, with characteristic bluntness: 'We had repeat offers by sheer consistency of our quality.' Chris Hancock adds that the 1990s was a good era for wine producers everywhere: 'Globally, in the '90s, you didn't have to *sell* wine: people *bought* it. It was this decade of optimism, of confidence, of money.'

While the UK market grew steadily during the first half of the decade, in the second half the export emphasis shifted to the United States. 'I think the most

THE HISTORY OF AUSTRALIAN WINE

WOLF BLASS®

Watch your sales soar with Wolf Blass

significant thing for the Australian wine industry,' says Bruce Tyrrell, 'was the '90 [Penfolds] Grange getting Wine of Year in the *Wine Spectator* [a US magazine, in 1995]. And what that did was, all over the world, suddenly we got taken seriously. And our top wines were taken as acceptable.'

This global rediscovery of Australian wine in the 1990s, particularly in almost-forgotten traditional markets such as Old Blighty, provoked a rush of blood to the heads of many winemakers and soon led to the oversupply that afflicted the Australian industry in the first decade of the twenty-first century. Brian McGuigan's assessment of the export boom, given in his interview in 2000, sums up the extreme sense of optimism of the time:

Of course, God gave us the main attribute that makes Australian wine sell and that is the fact that we've got the sunshine that makes the flavoursome wine … [But] Australian wine companies have been smart in the way in which they've made the wine. We've been clever in the way in which we've marketed the wine, established our image, built upon our image … So I've got great confidence in the future. Because when you go around the markets of North America, Europe or the UK, whilst you see a lot of our product, there's a lot more room for a lot more of it to be sent. And, of course, one mustn't forget that we Australians are pretty fortunate. Because the world does love Australians. We are seen as fun-loving, very open, honest and genuine people. And the product that we make is seen in the same way. As long as we all continue to deliver the same sort of service, and the same sort of passion in the product that we make and sell, I can't see that the vision that our industry has put forward to itself [will fail] … you can only look, really, to the next five or seven years, [and] the express train that we now see coming down that track is going to continue.

The 'vision' that Brian McGuigan refers to is the *Strategy 2025* document, unveiled at the inaugural Wine Australia exhibition in Sydney in 1996. The strategy's bold aim was to build the country's total wine sales to $4.5 billon—at least half of which would be exported—over the ensuing thirty years. Most industry commentators credit this bold vision with inspiring the subsequent boom in vineyard plantings and new wineries in the late 1990s and early 2000s.

One of the architects of 2025 was Len Evans, who describes how the plan was created:

Now, 2025 was very interesting. Brian Croser and I were in a hotel suite in 1995 and Croser was talking about will we get to a billion [dollars worth of export sales], yes or no, by 2000. At that time the indicators were not good. And I said, 'Well, it doesn't matter if we get to a billion or not. We're going to get to 800,

... the world does love Australians. We are seen as fun-loving, very open, honest and genuine people. And the product that we make is seen in the same way.
BRIAN McGUIGAN

THE HISTORY OF AUSTRALIAN WINE

850.' He said, 'The press will railroad us.' I said, 'I don't care. That's a huge advance. So it's a billion a year later, or two years later, who cares? What we should really be thinking about is the future and what we should be looking at is what do we need to say'—and I grabbed these things out of the air as I spoke; I mean, there was certainly no philosophical reason for doing it—I said, 'Let's say that we want to be in the top five or six [of the world's wine-producing countries in] thirty years' time. What would it take?' And Croser said, 'Well, very good. Let's find out.' So we spent some of the money of the Wine Foundation, of which I was chairman then [to research the figures, and said in the document] that by 2025, we had to do six or seven billion turnover, which put us in this category … Now, I'm talking about 2050 and I think that if Australia continues the way it is, maintains its integrity, does not become too complacent (there are signs that we are), then we should be in the top three.

Despite Evans' blithe admission of a lack of philosophical reasoning, *2025* turned out to be a hugely influential document. John Brown, of Brown Brothers, sums up the view of many:

It's marvellous what a good plan can do. It gives a whole lot of people the confidence to invest and it opens people's eyes to the possibilities when the work is done properly. I was a sceptic, along with many others, about the various benchmarks that were set in that strategy. For example, the billion dollars by the year 2000. It just seemed to be an impossible task but, as we know now, it was easily achieved. I think that the strategy was really instrumental in enabling the production capacity to meet the terrific export markets that are being achieved now. It brought a lot of new capital into the industry, a lot of new grape growing and a lot of new investment. It's really put Australia on the world's map. I'm a great believer in planning.

The 2025 vision wasn't wholeheartedly embraced by everyone, though. Some industry veterans sounded a note of caution, even as far back as 2000, at the height of the boom, when many of the interviews for this book were recorded. Karl Seppelt, for example, acknowledges that the success of the wine industry has been remarkable, thanks to its long-term planning, but also brings some valuable wisdom to the story:

Things take a long time to happen in this industry. And then they put together their 25-year plan … all the papers were put together, all the surveys were done and, surprisingly enough, they said that by the year 2000 we were going to crack the billion dollars, which we did. And they reckoned there'd be a million tons of grapes crushed, which is exactly right. And things are looking pretty rosy. All depending, of course, on our dollar, the overseas trade and the respect that we have in the various countries we're dealing with. But it's all pretty tough going and, while it looks good on paper, I don't know whether the cash flow's really as exciting as it ought to be ... So, one of the things that the industry has to learn to do is to get its prices up, and you can only do that by improving your image and generally working on it all the time. With the wine export councils and all the things they have, it can be done. As long as the industry works together, which it's been able to do now, I suppose, for ten or fifteen years—no fights ... And as long as everybody's working pretty well together, we'll keep on improving the situation. No doubt about that.

Of course, many in the industry now see that, since the turn of the century, Australian wine has become a victim of its export success: that super-cheap uber-brands such as Yellow Tail, first shipped to the United States in 2001, have radically cheapened the image of Brand Australia overseas. Many argue that the industry is now floundering partly because its sense of unity has unravelled. But they also argue that this is a necessary, if painful, stage in the development of Australia's wine culture: that it's important to accept that there are two industries—one focused on commodity wine and one devoted to fine wine.

Nevertheless, for Australian wine's old-timers, the remarkable change from virtually no exports in the 1960s to a huge and mostly vibrant export scene in the 1990s was a source of great pride and satisfaction. As Orlando's Keith Gramp says:

I was just thinking [about] how it's all changed with the export now ... Our main market before the [Second World] War was export and we were trying to get rid of the stocks ... [It's] good to see that at last we're back again with the export. And to think we've got it all around the world. I think that's one of the greatest things that has happened to the Australian wine industry—that we are now a country that produces wine [with a worldwide market]. And it's absolutely great that I am able to see that before I go away from this world ... We've certainly gone a long way.

Opposite: For many, this is the modern image of Australian wine overseas

THE HISTORY OF AUSTRALIAN WINE

THE LAST WORD: LEN EVANS

The best phone call I ever got was when I was at Bulletin Place [Len's legendary Sydney restaurant, an institution in the 1970s] and a bloke rang up and said, 'My name's Fred Crump from Isa Street, Cabramatta,' or something. I said, 'Yes, Mr Crump, what can I do for you?' And he said: 'I want to tell you, we have a barbecue every week, the whole street virtually, we take turns putting it on. And I've been reading some of your stuff, and I thought, this bloke obviously gets so much fun out of wine. So I stopped the beer keg. I didn't have a keg. I just had casks of wine, bottles of wine. And when the blokes arrived they said, Jesus Christ, what's this muck? You know. Anyway, they enjoyed it with their meat. That was a couple of years ago, and now we have Coonawarra tastings, Hunter tastings, and now we very, very rarely drink beer. Just because I thought: this Evans bloke is having so much fun, why can't I join that?' That's the phone call that pleases me most.

Opposite: Len Evans judging at the Adelaide Wine Show, 1988

ROGUES' GALLERY
The people who made it happen

The following people were interviewed between 2000 and 2003 for the National Wine Centre Oral History Project, 'Treading out the Vintage'. Rob Linn conducted the majority of the interviews and Lindsay Francis recorded some of the earlier interviews. The profiles here are based on the original biographies included with the recordings and transcripts held by the State Library of South Australia (www.slsa.sa.gov.au).

JOHN ANGOVE
Company patriarch, interviewed on 2 April 2003
Fourth generation member and current managing director of the well-known South Australian wine-making family business, Angoves, John was born in 1947 in Renmark in the Riverland. After leaving university in Adelaide, John spent eighteen months overseas, working at the Australian Wine Centre in London, and travelling through Europe for two vintages before coming home via the United States and joining the family company.

JACK BABIDGE
Cooper, interviewed on 6 February 2002
Born in 1913, Jack joined his family's barrel-making business after his father's death in 1936. Jack did business with all the families in the wine industry: the Wynns, Hamiltons, Seppelts, Angoves and Hardys. He retired in 1983, just when the family owners of wineries were relinquishing control to corporate managers.

BRIAN BARRY
Winemaker, interviewed on 4 April 2002
Born in Murray Bridge in 1927, Brian won a scholarship to Roseworthy to study oenology a year behind his brother, Jim. Dux of his class, Brian worked at Hamiltons Ewell winery, the Berri co-op and Stanley in Clare before planting riesling in Clare in 1977 for his own label and setting up as a consultant.

JIM BARRY
Winemaker, interviewed on 21 August 2002
Born in 1925, Jim studied oenology at Roseworthy before joining the Clarevale co-operative winery as assistant winemaker, becoming manager in the mid 1950s. While still working for Clarevale, Jim bought land north of Clare in 1959 and eventually established his own eponymous winery, assisted in the early days by legendary Wendouree winemaker Roly Birks.

ALEC BAXENDALE
Grape grower, interviewed on 27 June 2002
Alec grew up McLaren Vale in the 1930s surrounded by his parents' planting of unirrigated grenache, shiraz and doradillo grapes, used for fortified wines. After World War II he returned to McLaren Vale, bought a 50-acre block of the original Wirra Wirra property and grew cabernet and shiraz.

RAY BECKWITH
Wine scientist, interviewed on 23 June 2000
Arthur 'Ray' Beckwith graduated with first class honours in viticulture from Roseworthy in 1932 at the age of twenty. He was snapped up by Penfolds in 1934 to continue his groundbreaking work on cultured yeasts and went on to pioneer work on pH indicators to eliminate the problems of bacterial growth and spoilage, working alongside legendary winemakers Max Schubert and John Davoren. Beckwith was a member of the Australian Wine Institute, which was established in 1957.

JOHN BIRD
Winemaker, interviewed on 7 February 2003
In 1959, John left school at the age of sixteen to

become a laboratory assistant at Penfolds for 5 pounds a week, eventually working his way up to become the senior winemaker at Magill from 1970 to 1996. John played a large part in the development of Grange, but all the credit went to Max Schubert.

ROGER BLAKE

Winemaker, interviewed on 11 April 2003

Riverland-born son of a grape-grower, from 1948 Roger worked at a number of wineries including Tahbilk, McWilliams, Seaview and Kaiser Stuhl before settling in 1961 at Wynns, where he witnessed many new technological changes.

WOLF BLASS

Winemaker/personality, interviewed on 21 June 2000

After his childhood and early winemaking career in Germany during and after World War II, Wolf accepted an offer from Ian Hickinbotham at Kaiser Stuhl in 1961 to come to Australia and make pearl wine. After then working for Tolley, Scott & Tolley for three years he set out on his own, achieving national fame in 1974 when he won the Jimmy Watson trophy. In 1984 his company went public; he subsequently merged with Mildara before being taken over by Fosters.

JOHN BROWN JNR.

Winemaker, interviewed on 9 April 2003

The Brown Brothers winery was founded by John's great grandfather at Milawa, Victoria, with the first production of wine in 1889. His father, John Brown Snr., joined the winery in 1933 and John started in 1958. He was involved in vineyard expansion, including pioneering the cool-climate Whitlands vineyard; the establishment of an export market in 1972; and the development of the experimental 'kindergarten' winery.

ANDREW BULLER

Winemaker, interviewed on 10 April 2003

Born into a well-known Rutherglen winemaking family in 1957, Andrew's early memories were of playing in the winery. He went to Roseworthy from 1978 until 1981 and worked in Portugal, France and New Zealand before starting full-time with the family business.

GRANT BURGE

Winemaker, interviewed on 12 February 2003

Grant was the fifth generation member of a wine clan, but he never joined the family business. Instead, in 1977, at the tender age of twenty-five and after a stint at the Southern Vales co-op, he started South Australian Vintners with another young gun winemaker, Ian Wilson, eventually selling the successful Krondorf label to Mildara. In 1988, he started Grant Burge Wines and in 1999 bought back the Krondorf site in the Barossa Valley.

NOEL BURGE

Winemaker, interviewed on 7 February 2003

Grant Burge's uncle Noel was born in 1917 at Lyndoch where his family had vineyards. During the Great Depression, Noel's father established Wilsford Wines to make his own wine rather than sell his grapes for next to nothing. After completing Roseworthy, where he was one of the first oenology students, Noel worked at the Berri co-op before returning to the family farm.

COLIN CAMPBELL

Winemaker, interviewed on 10 April 2003

Born in Rutherglen in 1945, Colin is a fourth generation winemaker who studied oenology at Roseworthy when there were only eight in the course. In his first few years as winemaker in the 1960s, he witnessed enormous change and expansion: major replanting of vines, estate bottling and the region's first wine festival in 1967.

BEN CHAFFEY
Winemaker, interviewed on 5 March 2003
Four-year-old Ben arrived in Australia from California in 1918, the son of William Chaffey, one of two brothers invited by Prime Minister Deakin to pioneer irrigation settlements in Victoria. After completing the Roseworthy course in the mid 1930s, he started at the Emu Wine Company, blending fortified wine for export. After the war he bought the Seaview winery in McLaren Vale, and was the first in the area to bottle his own wine in the 1950s.

BILL CHAMBERS
Winemaker, interviewed on 9 April 2003
A fifth generation Rutherglen winemaker, the 25 year-old Roseworthy-trained Bill Chambers took over the reins at his family vineyard in 1958, where he built a formidable reputation for extraordinary fortified muscat and tokay. He started judging at wine shows in 1964 and built a formidable reputation in that field, too.

GORDON COLQUIST
Winery worker, interviewed on 12 February 2003
Gordon was born at Greenock in the Barossa in 1922. His father did boiler work for Penfolds and Gordon also started there in 1938. His general duties included walking Leslie Penfold Hyland's dogs but he eventually graduated to the cellars and the lab during the period when Max Schubert developed Grange.

DOUG CRITTENDEN
Wine merchant, interviewed on 26 November 2001
The son of a leading Melbourne grocer, Doug started work in his father's liquor shop in Toorak after World War II before going on a fifteen-month

trip to learn about the wine trade in Marseilles, Bordeaux and London. After his father died in 1954, Doug built the business into one of Australia's leading wine merchants, bottling sherry and table wines from many leading South Australian producers under the Crittenden label.

BRIAN CROSER
Winemaker, interviewed on 29 May 2003
Brian was born into a farming family in Millicent, in South Australia's south-east, in 1948. Tom Hardy supported the promising young student's trip to the University of California at Davis for three months before he started work at Hardys. Brian went on to become a lecturer at Charles Sturt Universty at Wagga Wagga, developing a winemaking course and building the university's winery in 1977, all before the age of thirty. He then established the Petaluma wine company and became heavily involved in wine-show judging and wine-industry politics.

TOM CULLITY
Winemaker/pioneer, interviewed on 25 July 2000
As a 22-year-old recently qualified doctor, Tom attended the first Barossa Vintage Festival in 1947 before starting a 40-year career as a physician in Perth. His passion for wine deepened during trips to Germany and France and through talking to Houghton winemaker Jack Mann in the 1960s. He established Margaret River's first commercial vineyard, Vasse Felix, in 1967, selling the property in 1985 to the Holmes à Court family.

DI DAVIDSON
Viticulturist, interviewed on 7 March 2002
Di grew up on a farm in Angas Plains, near Langhorne Creek. After studying agricultural science at Adelaide University, she worked as a tutor in botany at James Cook University. In 1975, she began working at Penfolds winery as a

wine chemist's assistant, later being promoted to a managerial position. In 1987, Di began her own viticultural consultancy.

FRANK DEVINE

Wine executive, interviewed on 15 March 2003
Frank was born in Brisbane in 1920. In 1955 he was employed as an office manager for the Wynn family, eventually becoming general manager. Wynns became a public company and in 1972 was taken over by Allied Vintners, who also owned Glenloth and Seaview Wineries and Tooheys Brewery. Frank stayed on and became a director of Tooheys.

MAX DRAYTON

Winemaker, interviewed on 5 May 2003
Drayton's and Tyrrell's are the oldest surviving family wineries in the Hunter Valley. Max was born in 1931 in Cessnock and lived and worked through many changes in the Hunter Valley, from the time when grape growers kept cattle to see them through the bad years to the growth of the region as a significant tourist area.

RAY DREW

Accountant and marketer, interviewed on 8 March 2002
Ray was born in 1922 in Adelaide. After World War II he became a bookkeeper, then an accountant, for Hardys Wines, when 90 per cent of the market was fortified. He became a founding member of the Beefsteak and Burgundy Club in 1954, and marketing director of Hardys in 1969.

PAM DUNSFORD

Interviewed on 31 December 2002
In 1973, at the age of twenty-two, Pam became the first woman admitted to Roseworthy Agricultural College to study oenology. She went on to do a Masters degree at The University of California,

Davis, in 1978, and worked at the Wynns winery in McLaren Vale from 1974 until 1986 before becoming winemaker at Chapel Hill in 1987.

DAVID DUNSTAN

Historian, interviewed on 29 November 2001
David was born in 1950 in New York where his father Keith was a foreign correspondent for Melbourne's *Herald and Weekly Times*. David developed an interest in wine from his father and his uncle Bill who bought wine from all over Australia during the 1960s. David has lectured widely and written many books about the history of Australian wine.

LEN EVANS

Writer, show judge, entrepreneur, interviewed on 6 May 2003
Born in Suffolk of Welsh parents, Len emigrated to New Zealand in 1953 at the age of twenty-two before ending up in Sydney, where his first job in the wine industry was as a glass washer at a hotel; he quickly worked his way up to assistant general manager. In 1962 he wrote the first wine column for the *Bulletin* before joining the Wine Board as national promotions executive. In 1967 he went independent, building a reputation as a writer with his 'Indulgence' column in the *Australian*, as a winery impresario with Rothbury in the Hunter and as a hugely influential wine show judge.

BERNIE GEHRIG

Winemaker, interviewed on 9 April 2003
Bernie's grandfather arrived in Australia in 1855 and bought a property in Rutherglen in 1867. By the time Bernie was born in 1940, the property consisted of 60 to 70 acres of vines. Initially, wine was only sold in barrels—9 to 40 gallons—and mainly dry red. White was not popular until the 1970s.

COLIN GRAMP

Technical director, interviewed on 26 June 2000

Colin's father, Hugo Gramp, along with Tom Hardy and Sydney Hill Smith, was one the three South Australian winemakers killed in the Kyeema air disaster in 1938. After studying oenology at Roseworthy, Colin joined the RAAF in 1942 and was demobbed in England in 1945. In California, on his way home, Colin picked up technical innovations that enabled Orlando to make and market Barossa Pearl, a light sparkling wine very popular in its day.

KEITH GRAMP

Marketer, interviewed on 4 July 2000

Like Colin, Keith is a direct descendant of Johann Gramp, who came to South Australia in 1837 and made his first riesling at Jacob's Creek in the Barossa Valley in 1850. Keith went to Roseworthy College for two years after World War II and then worked in marketing for the family company in Melbourne from 1949 to 1972.

DARYL GROOM

Winemaker, interviewed on 8 January 2003

Daryl enrolled at Roseworthy in 1976, finding a job with Kaiser Stuhl on graduation. That company was taken over by Penfolds in 1982, and Daryl remained with the company for a further twelve years, part of the team making Grange. In 1989, he moved to California to look after Penfolds' interests in the United States.

PERRY GUNNER

Wine executive, interviewed on 7 March 2002

Twenty-four-year-old Perry was an entomologist with the Department of Agriculture before he started working for the managing director of Orlando Wines in 1970. He became operations manager of Orlando's Rowland Flat winery in 1974 and managing director of the company in the mid 1980s.

JAMES HALLIDAY

Writer, winemaker, show judge, interviewed on 29 November 2001

James was born in 1938. He studied law and worked for Clayton Utz, eventually becoming managing partner. He was one of the founders, in 1970, of the Brokenwood winery in the Hunter, and went on to found Coldstream Hills in the Yarra Valley in 1985. Very much a protégé of Len Evans, James began judging wines in 1977 and wrote his first book in 1979. He retired from the law in 1988; Southcorp Wines took over Coldstream Hills in 1996.

NORMAN HANCKEL

Vineyard and production manager, interviewed on 19 June 2002

In 1948, the Roseworthy-trained 19-year-old Norman Hanckel became supervisor for all Seppelt vineyards in Australia. In 1957 he became the production manager at Yalumba, liaising with 400 grape growers, and in 1968 he moved to Hungerford Hill in the Hunter. After working for the NSW Department of Industrial Development, he set up his own winery, Camden Park, in 1977.

VALMAI HANKEL

Librarian, historian, writer, interviewed on 3 May 2001

Valmai's first job at the Public Library of South Australia was in the research service. In 1968 Hardys donated money to establish the Thomas Hardy Wine Library, and Valmai selected the publications. The Library's wine literature goes back to 1834. In the 1990s Valmai began writing articles about wine for newspapers and magazines.

CHRIS HANCOCK

Marketer, interviewed on 2 May 2003

After studying oenology at Roseworthy, Chris worked for Reynella, before joining Penfolds in

1964. Chris worked at Penfolds for twelve years, ending up in Adelaide as the production manager. In 1975 he joined Rosemount in a sales and marketing role as the winery expanded, becoming the biggest Australian producer of chardonnay by 1981. Chris was instrumental in the establishment of Rosemount in the UK market in 1983.

BILL HARDY
Winemaker, interviewed on 12 December 2001
Bill was born into the Hardy family clan in 1950. After university he went to Bordeaux to study winemaking, the first Australian to do so. He became the winemaker at Houghton in Western Australia in 1976 when the family bought the winery, and stayed there six years. Then, when Hardys bought the La Baume vineyard in France in the late 1980s, Bill took over its management from 1991 to 1994.

BOB HARDY
Winemaker, interviewed on 17 December 2001
Bob Hardy studied at Roseworthy in 1949 and in 1954 went to the Napa Valley, and also toured Europe. He returned to Australia via South Africa and started working as a Hardys winemaker in the Barossa at Dorrien before managing bottling and production at Mile End and Reynella.

RICHARD HASELGROVE
Winemaker, interviewed on 24 April, 8 May, 20 May, 2003
In 1949, at the age of thirteen, Richard began working in the school holidays at the Mildura Winery, where his father was winemaker. His uncle Colin was also involved in the industry and became managing director of Reynella. Richard worked two vintages in Bordeaux in the early 1960s before developing new wine brands for Mildara, eventually becoming chairman of the company before its takeover by Fosters in the 1990s.

PRUE HENSCHKE
Viticulturist, interviewed on 17 June 2002
Prue was born in Adelaide in 1951 and studied botany and zoology at Adelaide University. She met Stephen Henschke in 1973 and they married in 1975. After a trip to Geisenheim in Germany to study viticulture, and working in the Hunter Valley and at Roseworthy, Prue and Stephen joined Stephen's family business at Keyneton, bought land at Lenswood and planted a vineyard.

STEPHEN HENSCHKE
Winemaker, interviewed on 25 July 2002
Stephen was born in 1950 in Angaston. He grew up at Keyneton at his family's winery, which had started in the 1860s. He worked for Rothbury Estate in 1973 before travelling and working with his wife, Prue, returning to the family winery in the late 1970s. In 1982 he won the Arthur Kelman trophy in Sydney, the first of many awards. He began exporting wine in 1986.

IAN HICKINBOTHAM
Winemaker, restaurateur, writer, interviewed on 26 November 2001
Born in 1929, Ian studied oenology at Roseworthy, where his father Alan was deputy principal, then worked at Wynns in Melbourne running their laboratory. From the 1950s he worked at Wynns Coonawarra Estate, Tolleys in Hope Valley, and then Kaiser Stuhl as the technical manager. He introduced the 'bag-in-the-box' wine cask at Penfolds before buying Gini's restaurant in Toorak and writing for the *Financial Review*, the *Age* and *Winestate*.

ROBERT HILL SMITH
Winery owner, interviewed on 18 February 2003
Robert was born in Adelaide in 1951 into a wine-making family. He started at Yalumba in 1970 and travelled overseas in 1978 to learn about the wine

industry and to work vintage in France. In 1981 he took on the role of export manager, in 1983 marketing manager and finally, in 1985, managing director.

ALAN HOEY

Winemaker, interviewed on 26 August 2002
In the early 1960s Alan studied oenology at Roseworthy and worked at Stonyfell winery in his holidays. He obtained a cadetship with Glenloth Wines, which was then taken over by Seaview. In 1980 he moved to Yalumba as senior white-wine maker, working with Peter Wall on continuous fermentation for yeast culture.

DAVID HOHNEN

Winemaker, interviewed on 5 December 2002
David was born in Papua New Guinea in 1945. In 1968 he joined Stonyfell winery and studied oenology at Roseworthy and then at Fresno State College in the United States. He came back to Australia in 1972 and spent four years at Taltarni Winery in Victoria before planting the Cape Mentelle vineyard at Margaret River in 1976 and establishing Cloudy Bay in New Zealand in 1984.

BOB HOLLICK

Grape grower, interviewed on 1 April 2003
Bob grew up in the 1920s in Mildura where his father had a vineyard. He became involved with Mildara as one of their large-scale contract grape suppliers, became president of the Growers Association in Mildura and a member of the Australian Wine Board. He developed vineyards for Mildara in Coonawarra, Clare, Langhorne Creek and Margaret River in Western Australia and was an early adopter of mechanical pruning and harvesting machines.

IAN HOLLICK

Winemaker, interviewed on 28 April 2003
Ian was born in Mildura in 1950, studied agricultural science at Dookie in Victoria and worked for his uncle at Mildura vineyards in 1972. Ian designed the first mechanical pruner, studied in Bordeaux and set up his own business, Hollick Wines, in Coonawarra in 1984, winning the Jimmy Watson trophy in 1985.

DENIS AND TRICIA HORGAN

Winery owners, interviewed on 29 September 2001
Perth businessman Denis Horgan and his wife Tricia bought a farm in Margaret River in 1969. Californian wine legend, Robert Mondavi, encouraged them to plant a vineyard on the property. They initially planted 220 acres, the most significant vineyard in the Western Australia wine industry at that time. As well as establishing Leeuwin Estate, Denis also became a one-third owner of Petaluma with Len Evans and Brian Croser.

JIM INGOLDBY

Winemaker, interviewed on 7 February 2003
Jim's father owned Ryecroft Winery in McLaren Vale. Jim studied art and worked in an advertising agency before World War II, returning to make wine for Haselgroves. He established a McLaren Vale company to bottle wine and sold most of it to merchant Harry Brown in Sydney.

JOHN JAMES

Vineyard owner, interviewed on 25 July 2000
John's parents were publicans. He made his first wine when he was fourteen. He completed a degree in chemistry and, after visiting David Gregg at Margaret River in 1973, became interested in wine making. He purchased Ribbon Vale in 1977 and

planted 17 acres of grapes, working on the winery at weekends.

ROSS JENKINS

Winery executive, interviewed on 3 December 2002
In 1941, Ross started at Chateau Tanunda in the Barossa, then owned by Seppelt. He did clerical and laboratory work, and became manager in 1956, associate director in 1972, assistant general manager in 1975 and director in 1977.

ALEX JOHNSTON

Winemaker, interviewed on 11 May 2001
Alex was born in Adelaide in 1933, a descendant of the Johnstons, who established Oakbank brewery and bought land at McLaren Vale in 1892. Initially contract grape growers, from the early 1970s the Johnstons began to bottle wine under their own, Wytt Morro-designed Pirramimma label.

COLIN KIDD

Vineyard manager, interviewed on 5 March 2003
The son of a soldier settler vineyard owner, Colin started managing old vineyards for Lindemans in Coonawarra after World War II, later establishing new vineyards in Padthaway and eventually looking after all the company's vineyards. Colin also initiated what became known as South Australia's Vine Improvement Scheme.

RAY KIDD

Winemaker, executive, interviewed on 6 May 2003
Ray was born in Renmark in 1926 and his family had a vineyard. He was in the RAAF and then went to Roseworthy until 1948. He became the winemaker for Lindemans at Corowa in New South Wales, cellarmaster from 1951, director and general manager in 1962 and managing director in 1968.

PHILIP LAFFER

Winemaker, interviewed on 30 July 2002
Philip's father, Len, worked on wine research with John Fornachon, then lectured at Roseworthy until 1944. Philip studied at Roseworthy in 1958, joined Lindemans in 1963 as assistant winemaker to Ray Kidd, and moved quickly through the Lindeman's ranks, becoming chief winemaker. He then moved to Orlando and helped build Jacob's Creek into the huge brand it is today.

MAX LAKE

Vigneron, writer, polymath, interviewed on 29 June 2000
Max was born in New York in 1924 and came to Australia when he was three months old. He studied medicine and became a surgeon, working in Melbourne with Weary Dunlop. He started judging wine shows in the early 1960s, planted Lake's Folly vineyard in the Hunter in 1963, and wrote *Classic Wines of Australia*, one his many books, in 1966.

MERV LANGE

Winery owner, interviewed on 4 October 2001
Merv's father bought land at Frankland in 1946, cleared it and started farming. Merv married Judy in 1965 and they planted grapes in 1970. He made his first wine in 1975, and went to the Melbourne Expo in 1981 to market the wine outside Western Australia. He employed John Wade as winemaker in 1986.

PETER LEHMANN

Winemaker, interviewed on 22 June 2000
Peter was born in 1930, a fifth generation Barossa Lehmann. His father was a Lutheran minister. Peter left school in 1947 and became an apprentice winemaker at Yalumba, training under Rudi Kronberger. He stayed there for thirteen years, moving to Saltram as managing winemaker in

1959. He resigned in 1979 and developed his own business, Peter Lehmann Wines, in 1982.

IVAN LIMB
Wine businessman, interviewed on 26 March 2003
Ivan's grandfather made wine and brandy for Tolleys. Ivan was one of the five students to graduate from the new winemaking course at Wagga in 1975. His first job was at Orlando where he stayed until 1993, when he went on to form his own company, Australian Vintage, which he sold four years later for $120 million.

ROGER MACMAHON
Cork supplier, interviewed on 21 February 2002
Roger joined his father's cork import and manufacturing company in 1960. Leo Buring was a family friend and Roger had worked in many jobs before he joined the company: from selling corks to importing crystal.

FRANK MARGAN
Journalist, restaurateur, vigneron, interviewed on 3 May 2003
Frank became a cadet journalist at the *Mirror* in Sydney in 1947 and worked his way up to become news editor at the *Telegraph* when he was recruited to write for Len Evans at the Australian Wine Bureau in the 1960s. He then managed a hotel in Bali for three years, wrote a book called *The Grape and I* and planted grapes in the Hunter Valley.

BROTHER JOHN MAY
Winemaker, interviewed on 27 August 2002
Brother John joined the Jesuits in 1949 in Melbourne and transferred to the Sevenhill College and winery in the Clare Valley in 1963 with no background in the wine industry: in fact he was a non-drinker and had his first glass of wine with Jim

Barry in Clare. In 1972 he became the winemaker at Sevenhill, which is the only Jesuit commercial winery in the world.

BRIAN McGUIGAN
Wine businessman, interviewed on 27 June 2000
Brian's father Perc was the winemaker at Penfolds Dalwood in the Hunter. Brian started as a trainee winemaker at Magill for Max Schubert and Ray Beckwith, returning to Dalwood in the 1960s. In 1970 Brian bought Wyndham Estate with Digby Matheson and Tim Allen, going on to huge commercial success with traminer riesling. Wyndham was taken over by Orlando in 1990, so in 1992 he developed McGuigan Wines.

DON McWILLIAM
Winemaker, interviewed on 4 May 2003
In the 1950s and 1960s Don worked in all aspects of the industry at his family's vineyards, wineries and cellars. He and Karl Seppelt were elected to the Australian Wine Board in 1975 and lobbied for no increase in levies. They were instrumental in getting more funding for the Australian Wine Research Institute.

TOM MILLER
Horticulturist, interviewed on 13 June 2003
Tom was born in Perth in 1917. He joined the Department of Agriculture and worked in the apple industry, although he had a lot to do with Houghton winemaker Jack Mann and viticulturist Bill Jamieson. He moved to South Australia in 1955 where he became chief horticulturalist.

ROBIN MOODY
Winemaker, interviewed on 19 December 2002
Robin was sponsored by Penfolds to do the diploma course at Roseworthy. He worked at Magill and

Auldana before moving to the Allied Vintners group in Melbourne as division winemaker. He returned to Magill in 1994.

MICK MORRIS
Winemaker, interviewed on 9 April 2003
Mick was born in Rutherglen in 1928, fourth generation of a winemaking family with a history in the region that dates back to 1859. Mick was the first winemaker to be university educated, and his first vintage was in 1953. As well as continuing the family tradition of great fortified wines, Mick also introduced new styles of big red table wines.

DAVID MOSS
Horticulturist, interviewed on 17 March 2003
David started at the South Australian Department of Agriculture in 1949 as a fruit inspector. He moved to advisory work in 1956 at Mt Gambier, where he consulted on herbicides and vine selection and met many of the characters in the wine industry.

D'ARRY OSBORN
Winemaker, interviewed on 13 May 2001
Francis d'Arenberg (d'Arry) Osborn was born in 1926 in McLaren Vale. In 1943 he started work at his family's winery, assuming full control in 1957 after the death of his father. In 1978 d'Arry was awarded the Queen's Jubilee Medal, and an OAM in 2004 for services to the Australian wine industry and to the McLaren Vale region.

HARRY PALMER
Promoter, interviewed on 4 December 2002
In 1955, Harry was employed by the Australian Wine Board as a full-time promotions officer and eventually became general manager of the Board. As well as hiring a young Len Evans to spread the word, Harry also travelled widely, trying to open up export markets in the UK and the US.

BILL PANNELL
Vigneron, interviewed on 27 July 2000
Bill fell in love with wine while studying medicine in Perth in the 1960s. He planted the Moss Wood vineyard in 1969 in Margaret River and moved with his young family to Busselton as a doctor in 1970, sharing a practice with Kevin Cullen. In 1984 the Pannells sold Moss Wood to Keith and Claire Mugford and moved to Pemberton, where they set up more vineyards.

LEO PECH
Grape grower, interviewed on 3 July 2002
The son of a Barossa grape grower, in 1952 14-year-old Leo left school to help his father in the vineyard. In the early 1960s he became active in the Barossa grape-growers organisation and in the 1970s he was one of the first to replant his vineyard on rootstocks.

JOHN PENDRIGH
Wine executive, interviewed on 12 April 2001
John worked in the shipping industry before becoming general manager and chief executive of the Berri and Renmark co-operatives in the early 1980s. He went on to become chairman of the Australian Wine and Brandy Corporation and chairman of BRL Hardy after the co-ops merged with the old family wine company in 2003.

KEVIN PFEIFFER
Winemaker, interviewed on 2 April 2003
Kevin studied at Roseworthy in the early 1960s alongside Ian McKenzie, both of whom eventually went on to work in the Riverland's larger co-op wineries—Ian at Berri, Kevin at Loxton.

RON POTTER
Winemaker, inventor, interviewed on 22 August 2002
Ron graduated from the oenology course at Roseworthy in 1951 and worked as a winemaker for Miranda in Griffith before establishing an engineering business in 1963 to manufacture and market the Potter fermenter, a breakthrough in winemaking equipment that he'd invented himself. Ron also consulted for the establishment of the winemaking course at Charles Sturt University.

LEN POTTS
Vigneron, interviewed on 23 July 2002
Born in 1927 into the old Potts winemaking family of Langhorne Creek (established 1850), Len worked from a very young age in the vineyards and winery and has fond memories of a childhood spent fishing on the Coorong.

GUENTER PRASS
Winemaker, interviewed on 1 June 2000
Guenter arrived in Australia from Germany in 1955 to work for Orlando on their new, cool-fermented white wines. The 29-year-old wine technician had worked in France, Italy, Portugal, Spain and, crucially, in the hot grape growing regions of Morocco, Algeria, Tunis, Egypt and Lebanon. He went on to become managing director of Orlando.

BRYCE RANKINE
Wine scientist, educator, interviewed on 28 June 2000
Bryce studied in Adelaide, California and Stellenbosch and worked as a bacteriologist before joining the CSIRO's wine research group in 1950 and going on to become one of the most important figures at the Australian Wine Research Institute. He became head of the oenology course at Roseworthy in 1978, retiring in 1986 to consult and write books such as *Making Good Wine*, a seminal work for many in the industry.

BRUCE REDMAN
Winemaker, interviewed on 18 March 2003
Bruce's family had been making wine in Coonawarra for half a century when he was born in 1954. His father sold their winery, Rouge Homme, when Bruce was twelve, subsequently establishing Redman Wines in 1968. After working vintage around the world, Bruce returned to Coonawarra in 1981.

BOB ROBERTS
Winery owner, interviewed on 3 May 2003
Bob was born in Papua New Guinea in 1939 and moved to Sydney after World War II. He studied law but after meeting Len Evans bought a block of land in Mudgee and planted his Huntington Estate vineyard.

PHIL RYAN
Winemaker, interviewed on 5 May 2003
Phil joined McWilliams in 1965 at the age of nineteen, initially working in the company's laboratory and quality control department in Sydney. In 1978 he moved to the Hunter Valley to become a winemaker at Mount Pleasant, working under Maurice O'Shea's successor, Brian Walsh, finally becoming chief winemaker himself in 1985.

BETTY QUICK
Vineyard pioneer, interviewed on 5 October 2001
In 1959, at the age of twenty-one, Betty left nursing school in Fremantle to join her new husband on his farm in Western Australia's remote Mount Barker region. In 1966, the Forest Hill farm became the site of the first vineyard in the Great Southern, planted under a ten-year experimental lease with the

state government. Betty learned about viticulture from books and from talking to state viticulturist Bill Jamieson.

HERMANN SCHNEIDER
Chef, restaurateur, interviewed on 28 November 2001
Hermann, a young Swiss chef, arrived in Melbourne in 1956 to cook for the Swiss Olympic team. After the Games, Hermann stayed and opened his own restaurant, Two Faces, in South Yarra in 1960. The restaurant was a magnet for wine people such as Doug Crittenden, Max Lake and James Halliday.

KARL SEPPELT
Winemaker, interviewed on 28 June 2000
A member of the Seppelt family, whose winemaking history in the Barossa dates back to 1849, Karl studied oenology at Roseworthy in the 1950s before travelling to California in the 1960s, returning to the family firm as a passionate advocate for better clones of varieties such as pinot noir and chardonnay. Karl pioneered Seppelt's move into the then-new cooler-climate regions of Padthaway and Henty.

OLIVER SHAUL
Hotelier, restaurateur, interviewed on 30 June 2000
Oliver was born Ulrich Konrad in 1923 in Berlin. His family fled to Australia in 1939 and he joined the Australian army for a while before moving into a lifelong career in hotels and restaurants. He became managing director of the Federal Hotels group in 1951 and opened the world's tallest revolving dining room, The Summit, in Sydney in 1968.

FRANK SHEPPARD
Wine transporter, interviewed on 22 August 2002
After an apprenticeship on the South Australian Railways during World War II, Frank began work at Penfolds Magill winery in 1946 as an assistant to the engineer. In 1950 he started his own business transporting wine across the country in tankers.

KEITH SMITH
Winery executive, interviewed on 28 June 2002
Keith was born in Melbourne and trained in chemistry and management before becoming the managing director of the Kaiser Stuhl co-op in 1977. Under his management, Kaiser Stuhl acquired the Clarevale co-op and eventually merged with Penfolds.

BERNIE STEPHENS
Promoter, interviewed on 3 April 2003
Bernie's great, great grandfather, George Manning, was the first winemaker in McLaren Vale. After World War II Bernie was granted a War Service Land Settlement and developed a winery at Loxton, before moving to Adelaide as state manager of the Wine Information Bureau where he worked for twenty-one years.

VIV THOMSON
Winemaker, interviewed on 12 April 2003
After graduating from the oenology course at Roseworthy in the 1950s, fourth-generation vigneron Viv started work at his family's vineyard in Great Western, completing almost fifty vintages before handing over the reigns to his eldest son Ben in 2008.

GLADYS TINKLER
Vineyard owner, interviewed on 5 May 2003
Gladys is a descendant of the Matthews family, who settled in the Pokolbin Mountains and grew grapes in the 1800s, and of the Ingles family, who had a winery closer to Cessnock, on Ingles Lane.

She married Usher Gordon Tinkler, whose family started farming in the Hunter in 1844, and planted a vineyard in 1969 to supply grapes to McWilliams Mount Pleasant Winery.

DAVID TOLLEY

Vineyard manager, interviewed on 14 November 2001

A member of the Tolley winemaking family, David left school at eighteen, joined the navy and then worked for his father who had vineyards at Modbury, Tea Tree Gully and Hope Valley on the outskirts of Adelaide. These vineyards were compulsorily acquired by the government in the 1960s, so the Tolleys expanded into the Riverland and the Barossa where, in 1971, David planted cuttings of new varieties such as gewurztraminer and pinot noir.

REG TOLLEY

Winemaker, interviewed on 21 November 2001

Reg started work at his family's Hope Valley vineyards when he left school in 1945 and spent time at the winery and distillery his grandfather had established in the Adelaide suburb of Stepney in the 1800s. After the family sold their wine business in 1995 he set up a small vineyard in the Adelaide Hills.

HEC TREVENA

Vineyard owner, interviewed on 27 June 2000

Hec's family have been growing grapes in the Hunter since his father settled there after World War II and established a vineyard to supply the few wineries then in the valley with grapes. Hec inherited the vineyard when his father died in 1969.

GREG TROTT

Winery owner, dreamer, interviewed on 20 February 2003

Greg was born in 1934 on a McLaren Vale farm.

In 1969, after planting wine grapes on his family property and helping set up the Southern Vales co-op, he and his cousin Richard decided to renovate the crumbling old Wirra Wirra winery. He was a co-founder of the Bushing Festival in 1973 and a passionate supporter of the arts and his beloved region.

JAY TULLOCH

Winemaker, interviewed on 28 June 2000

Jay was born into a winemaking family in the Hunter Valley in 1944. The company was sold to Reed Consolidated in 1963, and Jay became general manger in 1975. He retired two decades later and then bought back the family business in 2001.

MARK TUMMEL

Winemaker, interviewed on 30 May 2001

Mark started as winemaker at Orlando in the Barossa in 1958 and became chief winemaker in the 1970s and technical director in the 1990s. He remembers very clearly the management buyout of Orlando in the 1980s and the subsequent sale to Pernod Ricard.

BRUCE TYRRELL

Winery owner, interviewed on 28 June 2000

Bruce, a fourth generation Tyrrell in the Hunter, was born in 1951 and joined the family winery in 1974. He set up the wine industry's first club for direct mail sales in 1978 and became CEO in 1994, going on to double the company's production.

JOHN VICKERY

Winemaker, interviewed on 22 June 2000

John studied oenology at Roseworthy in the early 1950s before joining Leo Buring and producing some legendary rieslings at Chateau Leonay in the Barossa in the 1960s and 1970s. After Leo Buring was taken over by Lindemans, John moved to the

Rouge Homme winery in Coonawarra, moving back to Leonay in 1993 when Orlando bought it and re-named it Richmond Grove.

NORM WALKER
Winemaker, interviewed on 21 March 2002
After studying at Roseworthy, Norm started work at Wynns Coonawarra Estate in 1954, then, following in the footsteps of his father, Hurtle, he became one of Australia's most influential sparkling winemakers, managing the Seaview Champagne Cellars for twenty-two years during the 1970s and 1980s.

PETER WALL
Winemaker and manager, interviewed on 22 August 2002
After graduating from Roseworthy in 1964, Peter started at Yalumba as an assistant winemaker, working his way up to wine and vineyard director. Peter was particularly interested in innovation and improvement, exploring the use of screwcaps in the 1970s and the planting of new varieties such as viognier in the 1980s and 1990s.

RAY WARD
Winemaker, interviewed on 23 June 2000
After returning from fighting in the jungles of Papua New Guinea during World War II, Ray studied oenology at Roseworthy and went on to work as a winemaker at Woodleys and Yalumba where, with Rudi Kronberger, he forged a reputation for excellent white wines.

BILL WIGNALL
Vineyard pioneer, interviewed on 7 October 2001
Bill was born in Fiji in 1930, studied as a veterinarian at Sydney University in 1947 and moved to Albany in Western Australia in the late 1960s, planting his first vines—cuttings he'd sourced from the Cullens in Margaret River in 1982.

NEIL WILKINSON
Viticulturist, interviewed on 4 December 2002
Orlando employed Roseworthy-trained Neil in 1963 to oversee their vineyards, liaise with growers and conduct research into new grape varieties in conjunction with the CSIRO. In 1968 Orlando sent Neil to California to observe mechanical harvesting.

GRAHAM WILTSHIRE
Winemaker, pioneer, interviewed on 13 May 2003
Graham planted the first vineyard in the Tamar Valley in 1966, and followed this with the Heemskerk vineyard in the Pipers Brook area in 1974. His sparkling wines attracted the interest of Louis Roederer Champagne, who went into partnership to produce Jansz sparkling wine in the late 1980s. Graham was also instrumental in the establishment of the Vineyards Association of Tasmania in 1974.

MORGAN YEATMAN
Winemaker, interviewed on 28 November 2002
Morgan grew up in the 1940s with wine on the table: his grandfather, a doctor, had owned a vineyard and sold grapes to the St Andrews winery in the Clare Valley. Morgan studied oenology at Roseworthy before making a name for himself as winemaker at Quelltaler and Glenloth in the 1960s and 1970s.

JOE ZEKULICH
Vineyard owner, interviewed on 26 July 2000
The oldest interviewee in this book, Joe was born in Croatia in 1907, the son of a grape grower, and migrated to Perth when he was sixteen. He started working in the wine cellars of the Croatian ex-pat community, before establishing his own vineyard in the Swan Valley and becoming an influential member of the grape-growing community.

NOTES

1 A Taste Revolution

1 Colin R Gramp, *The Barossa Pearl Story*, unpublished manuscript,
5 November 1966.

3 In the Winery

1 The title relates to a wine Not Exceeding 27% alcohol, thus NE27.

4 Men in White Coats

1 CG Bishop, *Australian Winemaking: The Roseworthy Influence*, Investigator
Press, Hawthorndene, SA, 1980, p. 9.

5 Migrants and Magpies

1 *Wine and Spirit News and Australian Vigneron*, 25 April 1919, p. 127.

8 Boom and Bust

1 Rob Linn, *Earth Vine Grape Wine: Yalumba & Its People*, Yalumba Wine
Company, Angaston, SA, 1999, pp. 115–22.

9 From Empire Port to Yellow Tail

1 Linn, ibid., p. 150.
2 www.awbc.com.au/winefacts/data/free.asp?subcatid=98

ACKNOWLEDGEMENTS

This major project could not have been possible without the full financial support and assistance of the Wolf Blass Foundation and the Winemakers Federation of Australia. Donations were also received from Robert Hill-Smith, Yalumba Wines and Treasury Wine Estate.

Individual involvement and thanks must go to Wolf Blass, chairperson and founder of the Wolf Blass Foundation, the past CEO of the Federation, Ian Sutton, and drivers behind the Foundation: Guenter Prass AM, past managing director of Orlando Wines; Stephen Millar AM, past managing director of Hardy's Wines; Paul Clancy OAM, former publisher and proprietor of Winetitles Australia; and present CEO of the Winemakers Federation of Australia, Stephen Strachan. Also Mrs Judi Prosser, secretary of the Wolf Blass Foundation.

The major task of first interviewing over two hundred living pioneers associated with the Australian wine industry, and then transcribing and editing each of those individual stories, was conducted by the historian Rob Linn.

Special gratitude goes to director of The Author's Agent, Averill Chase, and to managing editor of Melbourne University Publishing, Diane Leyman.

PICTURE CREDITS

p. ii Yalumba **p. v** Courtesy of Yvonne Vaughan/Yalumba **pp. vi–vii** Courtesy of James Halliday/Treasury Wine Estates **p. x–xi** Sievers Wolfgang/National Library of Australia [2512660] **p. xii** Bonnie Savage Photography **p. 2** Photo by News Ltd, Sydney/Yalumba **p. 5** Newspix/Stuart Mcevoy **p. 6** Bonnie Savage Photography **p. 9** From *Wine—Australia*, provided courtesy of Wine Australia (formerly Australian Wine & Brandy Corporation) **p. 12** Image courtesy of the State Library of South Australia [PRG 1453/62/92] **p. 13** Images courtesy Wytt Morro **p. 14** Image courtesy of the State Library of South Australia [BRG 330/9/A72] **p. 15** top: Sievers Wolfgang/National Library of Australia [3416410]; bottom: Image courtesy of the State Library of South Australia [BRG 233] **p. 16** left: Image courtesy of the State Library of South Australia [PRG 280/1/6/167]; right: Image courtesy of the State Library of South Australia [BRG 330/9/A72] **p. 17** Image courtesy of the State Library of South Australia [BRG 330/9/A72] **p. 19** Image courtesy of the State Library of South Australia [PRG 1453/62/9] **p. 21** Image courtesy of the State Library of South Australia [BRG 330/9/A72] **p. 23** Image courtesy of Royal Agricultural & Horticultural Society of South Australia Incorporated **p. 26** Bonnie Savage Photography **p. 29** Adrian Matthiassen/iStock Photo **p. 30** Image courtesy of Brown Brothers **p. 31** Image courtesy of the State Library of South Australia [BRG 330/9/A72] **p. 32** Image courtesy of the State Library of South Australia [B 58973/76] **p. 34** Image courtesy of the State Library of South Australia [PRG 1453/62/35] **p. 35** Yalumba **pp. 36–37** Image courtesy of the State Library of South Australia [PRG 280/1/45/181] **p. 39** Image courtesy of the State Library of South Australia [PRG 1543/62/42] **p. 41** Image courtesy of Leeuwin Estate **p. 43** Yalumba **p. 45** Image courtesy Best's Wines **p. 46** Bonnie Savage Photography **p. 49** Yalumba **p. 51** Image courtesy of Bill Hardy, Hardy Wine Company **p. 52** left: Image courtesy of the State Library of South Australia [PRG 1453/62/39]; right: Image courtesy of the State Library of South Australia [PRG 1453/62/38] **p. 53** Image courtesy of the State Library of South Australia [PRG 1453/62/40] **p. 55** left: Image courtesy of the State Library of South Australia [PRG 1453/62/31]; right: Image courtesy of the State Library of South Australia [PRG 1453/62/32] **p. 56** top: Yalumba; bottom: Yalumba **p. 59** Image courtesy of the State Library of South Australia [PRG 1453/62/37] **p. 60** top: Wolf Blass; Below: Angove Family Winemakers **p. 61** Angove Family Winemakers **p. 62** Yalumba **p. 64** Image courtesy of Royal Agricultural & Horticultural Society of South Australia Incorporated **p. 65** Wolf Blass **p. 67** Image courtesy of Yellow Tail **p. 68** Bonnie Savage Photography **p. 71** National Archives of Australia [Barcode 9722158] **p. 73** top: Image courtesy of the State Library of South Australia [BRG 330/9/A72]; bottom: Image courtesy of Mark Hamilton/Hamilton's Ewell Vineyards **p. 75** Courtesy of Bill Hardy, Hardy Wine Company **p. 77** Yalumba **p. 78** National Archives of Australia [Barcode 5984732] **p. 81** Image courtesy of the University of Adelaide [S.986] **p. 83** Image courtesy of the State Library of South Australia [B 59959] **p. 84** top: Image courtesy of Cullen Wines; bottom: Yalumba **p. 85** top: Image courtesy of Royal Agricultural & Horticultural Society of South Australia Incorporated; bottom: Image courtesy of C A Henschke & Co **p. 86** Bonnie Savage Photography **p. 89** Bonnie Savage Photography **p. 90** Wolf Blass **p. 95** Image courtesy of Penfolds **p. 96** Image courtesy of Cloudy Bay Vineyards **p. 99** Mick Rock/Cephas **p. 101** Images courtesy Wytt Morro **p. 102** Sievers Wolfgang/National Library of Australia [4803012] **p. 103** Angove Family Winemakers **pp. 104–105** Image courtesy of Brown Brothers **p. 106** Bonnie Savage Photography **p. 109** From *The Grapes are Growing*, provided courtesy of Wine Australia (formerly Australian Wine & Brandy Corporation) **p. 112** Image courtesy of Picardy Wines **p. 115** Image courtesy of Dr Garry Cullity **p. 116** Image courtesy of Graham Wiltshire **p. 117** Image courtesy of Graham Wiltshire **p. 119** Image courtesy of Mount Mary Vineyard **p. 123** Photography by Televin Photographers, Tanunda/Yalumba **p. 124** Wolf Blass **p. 125** left: Photography by Advertiser Newspapers Ltd/Yalumba; right: Image courtesy of Coonawarra Vignerons Association **p. 126** Bonnie Savage Photography **p. 129** Image courtesy of Bill Hardy, Hardy Wine Company **p. 130** Yalumba **p. 131** National Archives of Australia [Barcode

8888688] **p. 133** Wolf Blass **p. 137** National Archives of Australia [Barcode 5981731] **p. 140** Image courtesy of the State Library of South Australia [BRG 330/9/A72] **p. 141** left: Yalumba; right: From *Wine—Australia*, provided courtesy of Wine Australia (formerly Australian Wine & Brandy Corporation) **p. 142** Image courtesy of Leeuwin Estate **p. 144** State Library of Victoria [H2005.100/1134] **pp. 146–147** Image courtesy of Mount Mary Vineyard **p. 148** Bonnie Savage Photography **p. 151** Yalumba **p. 152** Image courtesy of Royal Agricultural & Horticultural Society of South Australia Incorporated **p. 153** Image courtesy of Bill Hardy, Hardy Wine Company **p. 155** Image courtesy of the State Library of South Australia [BRG 330/9/A72] **p. 159** Wolf Blass **p. 161** From *Wine—Australia*, provided courtesy of Wine Australia (formerly Australian Wine & Brandy Corporation) **p. 163** Image courtesy of the State Library of South Australia [BRG 330/9/A72] **p. 164** Photography by Advertiser Newspapers Ltd/Yalumba **p. 165** top: Wolf Blass; bottom: Photography by Telvin Photographers, Tanunda/ Yalumba **pp. 166–167** Wolf Blass **p. 168** Bonnie Savage Photography **p. 171** Yalumba **p. 173** Images courtesy of Bill Hardy, Hardy Wine Company **p. 174** left: Image courtesy of the State Library of South Australia [BRG 330/9/A72] **p. 175** Image courtesy of the State Library of South Australia [BRG 330/9/A72] **p. 179** Wolf Blass **p. 183** Image courtesy of Yellow Tail **p. 185** Image courtesy of Royal Agricultural & Horticultural Society of South Australia Incorporated **p. 186** Image courtesy of the State Library of South Australia [BRG 330/9/A72]

INDEX